PARENTING THE YOUNG ADULT YEARS

—❖—

Maintaining Strong Family Ties and
Healthy Relationships with Your Emerging
Adult Children

© **Copyright 2024 - All rights reserved.**

The content contained within this book may not be reproduced, duplicated or transmitted without direct written permission from the author or the publisher.

Under no circumstances will any blame or legal responsibility be held against the publisher, or author, for any damages, reparation, or monetary loss due to the information contained within this book, either directly or indirectly.

Legal Notice:

This book is copyright protected. It is only for personal use. You cannot amend, distribute, sell, use, quote or paraphrase any part, or the content within this book, without the consent of the author or publisher.

Disclaimer Notice:

Please note the information contained within this document is for educational and entertainment purposes only. All effort has been executed to present accurate, up to date, reliable, complete information. No warranties of any kind are declared or implied. Readers acknowledge that the author is not engaged in the rendering of legal, financial, medical or professional advice. The content within this book has been derived from various sources. Please consult a licensed professional before attempting any techniques outlined in this book.

By reading this document, the reader agrees that under no circumstances is the author responsible for any losses, direct or indirect, that are incurred as a result of the use of the information contained within this document, including, but not limited to, errors, omissions, or inaccuracies.

CONTENTS

INTRODUCTION 1
    Defining the Young Adult Years (18–25) 1
    Understanding the Transition From Childhood to Adulthood 2
    Understanding the Transition From Parent to Guide 4
    The Importance of Maintaining Strong Family Ties 5
    Setting Goals for Healthy Relationships 7

CHAPTER 1: COMMUNICATING WITH YOUR ADULT CHILDREN .. 9
    Respecting Their Autonomy and Choices 10
    Active Listening 14
    Sharing Wisdom Instead of Giving Advice 17
    Avoid Criticism 21

CHAPTER 2: ESTABLISHING BOUNDARIES WITH LOVE AND RESPECT 27
    Encouraging Open Conversations 28
    Financial Responsibilities 29
    Instilling Values of Responsibility 30
    Encouraging Emotional Resilience 31
    Respecting Privacy 33
    Being Available for Support 34
    Maintaining an Open Line of Communication 35
    Establishing Boundaries With Love and Respect 36

CHAPTER 3: FOSTERING INDEPENDENCE AND RESPONSIBILITY 41
    Teaching Your Young Adult Financial Skills 41
    Encouraging Self-Care and Well-Being 47
    Physical Health 50
    Developing Decision-Making and Problem-Solving Skills 55

CHAPTER 4: SUPPORTING EDUCATIONAL AND CAREER PATHS .. 57
    Understanding the Challenges Faced by Young Adults 58
    Career Challenges Young Adults Face 62
    How to Foster a Supportive Environment for Your Young Adult 63

Navigating the Decision-Making Process With Your Young Adult Children 66
Letting Your Child Lead: Trusting Their Choices 68
Dealing With Failure and Setbacks 70
The Art of Letting Go (While Still Being There) 71

CHAPTER 5: NAVIGATING CONFLICT AND DIFFICULT CONVERSATIONS 73

Getting the Right Mindset 75
Identify Triggers 76
Have Realistic Expectations 77
Productive Dialogue, Active Listening, Negotiation 80
Some Other Tips for Managing Conflict 82
Rebuilding trust 85
The End Goal 87

CHAPTER 6: DEALING WITH SETBACKS IN YOUR ADULT CHILD'S LIFE 89

Parental Instincts 89
Offering Parental Guidance 91
Job-Searching Assistance 93
Balancing Support With Independence 96
Setting Realistic Expectations 98
Encouraging Self-Care 101

CHAPTER 7: MAINTAINING STRONG FAMILY TIES THROUGH ACTIVITIES AND TRADITIONS 105

Prioritize Regular Quality Time 106
Cultivate and Uphold Family Traditions 109
Include Adult Children in Decision-Making 111
Nurture Sibling Relationships 113
Support Their Major Milestones 115
Use of Technology When Physically Distant to Maintain Connections 117

CONCLUSION 121

REFERENCES 127

INTRODUCTION

—❖—

As children move from dependents to independent individuals, your role as guardians changes from being their parents to becoming their guides and even their friends. It's a radical transformation that may take several years. In your eyes, they are still young, innocent children who need proper care and regular parenting. Their physical growth spurt may be the only outward change you notice, and you might not be fully aware of what mental changes are taking place.

Sometimes, children find it difficult to deal with their growth spurts, both mentally and physically. These spurts change their behavior toward you and others. Depending on parenting methods, it may escalate and lead to strained relationships in the family, which can fester with time.

However, it's no one's fault. It's a generational problem as old as time. This book covers many common issues and lays out some effective solutions so you can keep a happy and fulfilling relationship with your young adults.

Defining the Young Adult Years (18–25)

The young adult years refer to the stage of life between adolescence and full adulthood, roughly spanning ages between 18 and 25. This period is characterized by significant personal, social, and psychological development as your children transition from dependency to independence and establish their identities, careers, and relationships.

Take yourself back to when you were 18. You were fresh out of high school or in the final months. A world of possibilities opened up before you. You had come of age, mastered driving, started (seriously) thinking about your future, begun to act on your romantic feelings, and were busy making new friendships or studying late hours.

You also started making certain decisions on your own, became more rebellious, experimented with new things, tried to deal with your physical and mental changes, and ended up more confused than you ever were. Dig deeper and think about the memories you might have blocked out. Do you remember lashing out at your parents, doing the exact opposite of what they told you to do, even though you didn't want to do it? How about questioning their decisions at every step?

Young adults today experience similar highs and lows in their lives, but as a parent, their highs might be hard to keep pace with, and their lows can be things you had never even thought about. Life changes and each generation faces the same issues but in different packaging.

Understanding the Transition From Childhood to Adulthood

The transition from childhood to adulthood can be taxing for your child. Many factors are involved in it. These include:

- **Identity formation:** Young adults explore various aspects of their identity, including their values, beliefs, sexual orientation, and career aspirations. This exploration may involve trying out different roles and lifestyles to discover what feels authentic.

- **Education and career:** They pursue higher education or vocational training during this time to gain the skills and qualifications needed for their chosen careers. This period may also involve job hunting, internships, or entry-level positions as they establish themselves professionally.

- **Independence:** This post-adolescence period is marked by a growing sense of independence from you, the parent. They may move out of childhood homes, establish their own households, and take on responsibilities like paying bills, managing finances, and making decisions about their own lives.

- **Relationships:** This stage often involves starting intimate relationships, whether romantic or platonic. Young adults may explore dating, friendships, and long-term partnerships as they seek companionship, support, and emotional fulfillment.

- **Personal growth:** Young adulthood is a time of personal growth and self-discovery. Your children may confront challenges, make mistakes, and learn from their experiences as they navigate the complexities of adulthood.

- **Socialization:** They often engage in social activities and communities that reflect their interests and values. This may include joining clubs or organizations, participating in recreational sports or hobbies, or attending social events and gatherings.

In a nutshell, young adult years are a time of transition, growth, and exploration as your children embark on the journey toward adulthood and begin to shape their own lives and futures.

Understanding the Transition From Parent to Guide

From your perspective, your child's young adulthood is equally taxing, but your transition process is very different from theirs. You need to assume the role of a guide instead of a parent. It will help you be a part of your adult children's growth, nurture their independence, and build a thriving relationship that will last for life.

- As children grow older, it's essential to encourage their independence. Imagine that your parents hadn't changed how they treated you from child to adult, like groundings, consequences, restrictions, and so on. You wouldn't have responded positively to their controlling behavior as an adult. Your children may not be fully grown adults yet, but they are almost there. To treat them like adults, you should give them their independence.

- You need to respect them the way they respect you. It won't happen until you become their mentor and guide instead of an authoritative parent.

- Instructing them doesn't give them space to think on their own. They need to develop their identity and establish their independence, and being their guide will give them enough space to do that.

- As a parent, you think of your adult children as kids. If you embrace the role of a guide, you will automatically imagine them as adults and equals. This change in perception will make it easier for you to give them all the necessary tools for adulthood.

- As your children mature, conflicts with them may escalate. That is primarily because of your parenting. You will notice a significant decline as soon as you switch to guidance.

- Have they been hiding things or lying to you lately? It may happen because young adults are not comfortable sharing certain things with their parents, like romantic relationships or problems. But they can learn to share them with their guide.

The Importance of Maintaining Strong Family Ties

Family ties aren't ropes binding people together in forced harmony. A family tie is a feeling of belonging that arises from a shared past, years of memories, and countless moments of love. However, as time passes, these strong ties may begin to fade, especially during your children's young adult years. They (or you) may not realize the importance of this bond until it is too late.

- **Emotional support:** Families provide a support system during both good times and bad. They offer emotional support, comfort, and encouragement during difficult times, helping your children cope with stress, grief, or other challenges.

- **Sense of belonging:** Strong family ties foster a sense of belonging and identity. When your children believe their family cares for and accepts them no matter what, they will have healthy confidence and self-esteem.

- **Values and traditions:** Families often pass down values, beliefs, and traditions from one generation to the next. These cultural and familial traditions help your children understand their heritage and create a sense of continuity and connection with their roots.

- **Socialization and development:** Families play a vital role in socializing children and teaching them essential life skills, such as communication, problem-solving, and conflict resolution. Positive family relationships contribute to healthy emotional development and interpersonal skills.

- **Mutual support and collaboration:** You and your children can collaborate and support each other in achieving common goals, whether they are related to education, career, or personal development.

- **Stability and resilience:** Strong family ties provide a foundation of stability and resilience, helping your children weather life's ups and downs. Knowing they have a supportive family to fall back on can give them the confidence to take risks and pursue their goals.

- **Health and well-being:** Sociology experts Patricia A. Thomas, Hui Liu, and Debra Umberson have proven that strong family connections are linked to better physical and mental health. Close family relationships can reduce the risk of depression, anxiety, and other mental health issues, as well as promote healthier lifestyle choices.

- **Intergenerational support:** Families often provide intergenerational support, with members of different generations helping each other in various ways. This support can range from childcare and eldercare to financial and emotional support.

Setting Goals for Healthy Relationships

Maintaining your bond with your children becomes all the more critical during their young adult years. Their sense of independence and other factors may mean they begin to drift away. In addition to their evolving relationships at college and the workplace, your connection might take the sidelines. Here are some reasons why setting goals will be beneficial for your relationship:

- Establishing clear goals gives your adult children something to aspire to.

- It keeps them determined to improve their relationship with you.

- It helps you understand their aspirations so you can work together to achieve them.

- It provides an opportunity to discuss values and expectations, making you open up to each other and communicate better.

- You can hold each other accountable for doing something that doesn't agree with your goals, like your children falling prey to a bad habit.

When you have shared goals in your parent-young adult relationship, you will have many chances to work together and strengthen your bond.

CHAPTER 1:

Communicating with Your Adult Children

———❖———

Proper communication is the key to healthy relationships with your young adult children. Without it, your bond of almost two decades will disintegrate into hostility and resentment. Talking with them authoritatively may also negatively affect your relationship. Remember, they are your children, but they aren't children anymore. They are adults with a sense of independence and responsibility.

You cannot advise them like preteens, instruct them like preschoolers, or mollycoddle them like toddlers. On the other hand, you cannot be too indulgent or be a pushover either. The trick lies in striking a balance between parenting and being a friend. The idea is to communicate like a trusted guide.

Overindulgence in their childhood may have brought you closer together in the past, but if you continue this style of parenting into adulthood, you are at risk of disempowering them from being able to make decisions for themselves. Similarly, authoritative parenting (loving but firm) may have worked wonders in their preteens but could elicit exactly the opposite behavior to what you were hoping for. The fine line between the two styles is possible. It just takes understanding and work.

Respecting Their Autonomy and Choices

Young adults prize their ability to make their own choices since they were generally not allowed to do so as children. Effective communication involves respecting autonomy. Trust your parenting and your child's ability to make decisions independently. Even if you think they are wrong, give them time to realize it themselves. Don't give them advice unless asked.

There may be a chance your child keeps making the wrong choices without learning from their mistakes, but if you keep disciplining or reminding them of their past mistakes, you will push them deeper into the void. The benefits of respecting their choices far outweigh the cons.

- **Enhanced communication:** Pediatric experts Christina Han and Mariana Brussoni have conducted extensive studies to prove that positively supporting a child's autonomy affects their independence and growth. Respecting your children's autonomy encourages open and honest communication. They will feel more comfortable discussing their thoughts, feelings, and experiences with you because you see and behave with them as adults.

- **Mutual respect:** Respecting autonomy demonstrates trust and respect between parents and young adults. This mutual respect lays the foundation for a more equal and balanced relationship where both you and your children feel valued and heard.

- **Increased trust:** Granting autonomy implies you trust them to carve their own path. In turn, they will begin to trust you as they open up to you more often. This will eventually strengthen your relationship since it is built on honesty and transparency.

- **Empowerment:** Supporting their choices will empower them to take control of their lives and make decisions that fit their values and goals. They will be more careful in their choices so as not to disappoint you. This sense of empowerment and care will boost their confidence and self-esteem.

- **Healthy boundaries:** Establishing healthy boundaries within the parent–young adult relationship is essential. Respecting your children's choices helps you recognize the importance of allowing them to assert their independence while still providing guidance and support when needed.

- **Supportive environment:** When parents respect their young adult's autonomy, they create an environment where their child feels free to express themselves and pursue their interests without fear of judgment or criticism.

- **Promotes independence:** This is a direct benefit that makes your children independent and self-reliant. They make decisions and learn to take responsibility for their actions, developing essential life skills that will serve them well in adulthood.

- **Conflict resolution:** Respecting their autonomy teaches them how to resolve conflicts and negotiate differences on their own. They learn to communicate their needs and preferences assertively while also considering the perspectives of others. It helps them take control of their lives and become better leaders.

Parents who respect their children's autonomy are positive role models for healthy relationships. Observing your behavior will teach children valuable lessons about respect, empathy, and compromise.

Did you know the bonds forged between the ages of 18 and 25 are more likely to last for a lifetime? A parent–child relationship built on mutual respect and autonomy will withstand the challenges of adulthood and beyond. It lays the groundwork for a solid and enduring bond that evolves as your children grow and mature.

How to Respect Their Autonomy to Encourage Better Communication

Respecting your children's autonomy doesn't mean you let them do what they want. You need to show your support for their choices and assure them that you stand beside them if something goes wrong. If you have conflicting views on a subject, share your side of the story instead of dismissing your children's opinions. They need to understand why you aren't thinking on the same plane.

Encourage them to think about differing opinions. As time passes, they will feel more comfortable sharing their ideas and actions with you, no matter how radical or tangential they may be. Additionally, if you are controlling their decisions, they may not respond positively. Offer guidance and support instead. Empower them to make their own decisions and learn from their experiences. Instead of saying, "You should not have done that," ask them how you can help resolve their situation and provide guidance if they cannot come up with a solution on their own.

Take the Initiative to Talk

Young adults are usually distant with their parents. Take the initiative to open communication by asking simple questions like, "How was your day?" or "What did you have for lunch?" Don't discipline or taunt them for having junk food. Criticism is not going to get you anywhere. Instead, you could express your desire to have been able to join them.

Acknowledge Their Independence

Recognize and celebrate their growing independence and decision-making abilities. Appreciate even their smallest decisions, like helping a friend with their coursework. Let them know you support their choices with simple congratulatory words like, "Great work!" or "Good decision!"

Coming of Age Boundaries

Establish clear boundaries that respect your children's autonomy and the family's values. Negotiate boundaries together if they have reached the legal drinking age, and discuss what is acceptable at home. Let them know the consequences of excessive drinking and set limits.

Respect Their Privacy

Respect their privacy by not invading their personal space or snooping into their private matters without permission. Trust is essential in developing autonomy and keeping communication honest with your young adult.

Be there to offer support and guidance whenever it's needed, but let them take the lead in seeking help or advice. Support their independence by empowering them to seek solutions on their own. Validate their feelings and emotions, even if you may not always agree with their decisions. Let them know that even if you don't agree with their thoughts, you can respect their choices.

Active Listening

Active listening is a critical part of effective communication. Say your young adult is always eager to talk to you. One evening, they describe their day while you are pretending to listen. Out of the blue, they ask about your thoughts on the subject, but since you don't know what they were on about, you say something generic like, "Yeah, it's good!"

They aren't children anymore, so they will instantly realize you weren't listening to them. The next time, they may not be so eager to talk to you about anything at all, which will ruin your relationship with them.

The Benefits of Active Listening

The biggest benefit of active listening is improved communication. It enhances the quality of communication by ensuring that both you and your children feel understood and respected. They are more likely to open up and share their thoughts and feelings when they feel heard.

Subsequently, greater and more nuanced communication leads to healthier relationships. When your children feel heard and understood, it deepens your connection with them. They realize you are interested in what they have to say, which will strengthen the bond between you two.

While your adult children won't seek solutions from you directly when they share a problem, they usually expect you to come up with a solution. If you're listening actively, your greater experience and knowledge will, more often than not, help you find the right solution. Other benefits of active listening are:

Increased Empathy

Active listening will allow you to put yourself in your child's shoes, leading to greater empathy and compassion. You will know precisely when to say you understand their dilemma or that you can see how it might have affected them. That empathy can improve your relationship with them and make them more comfortable talking to you.

Greater Productivity

At their age, all your child needs is to be heard. Their emotional turmoil will be reduced if they can simply talk about their problems with someone. That is probably the only thing standing in the way of their studies or work.

Personal Growth

Listening to your children sets an example for them. They will also learn to listen actively to other people, leading to their personal growth. By being open to others' perspectives and feedback, they'll better understand their behaviors and beliefs, leading to continuous improvement and development.

Improved Mental Health

The knowledge that they are being listened to and understood can have a calming effect on young adults, reducing stress and promoting mental well-being. Active listening creates a supportive environment where they feel valued and validated, leading to a more positive emotional state.

The Art of Active Listening

You may be wondering, *Isn't active listening the same as listening?* No, there are many differences between the two. When you say that a person is listening, they may simply be hearing, not understanding. Active listening involves hearing, understanding, and showing that you understand. Here's how you can master this art and actively listen to your children to improve your relationship:

Giving Full Attention

Active listening requires giving your full attention to the person speaking to you. It means putting aside distractions like your phone, work, or other thoughts and focusing solely on what is being said.

Demonstrating Interest

Show them that you are interested and engaged in what they are saying through your body language, like maintaining eye contact, nodding occasionally, and using facial expressions to convey interest. For instance, if your child is narrating a shocking incident (though it may not be shocking to you), shake your head with eyes open wide and punctuate their pauses with, "Really?" or "What happened next?"

Reflecting and Paraphrasing

Reflect back on what they said by paraphrasing their words or summarizing their main points. Doing this demonstrates that you are actively processing the information and helps to clarify any misunderstandings.

Asking Clarifying Questions

If something is unclear or you need more information to understand your child's message fully, don't hesitate to ask clarifying questions. This shows you are genuinely interested in understanding their perspective. For example, "What was it you said earlier?" or "How did that happen?"

Providing Feedback

Offer feedback to your children to let them know you understand their message. It shouldn't be judgmental or harsh. Verbal affirmations like, "That makes sense," or nonverbal cues like nodding or smiling would get your message across.

Ideally, you should suspend judgment and refrain from interjecting your own opinions while your children are talking. Instead, focus on listening with an open mind and seeking to understand their point of view.

Avoid interrupting their narration unless necessary. They are in the flow of things, and interruptions will break their chain of thought. Make a mental note of any doubts you wish to clarify. If you cannot understand what's being said next without clarification, apologize, excuse yourself, and then ask.

Sharing Wisdom Instead of Giving Advice

On the surface, sharing wisdom and experiences may seem like giving advice, but in reality, they are worlds apart. Giving advice means directly providing suggestions or solutions to problems. Sharing wisdom involves discussing your experiences and letting your children pick up possible lessons or solutions.

Advice can often seem judgmental, and young adults don't like being judged. Their sense of independence will prompt them to come up with solutions. Though you are giving advice with the best will in the world, they might not take it in that spirit.

You need to teach them without being direct and preachy. They know they have a lot to learn, but they may not take your advice kindly. Subtly sharing your wisdom and experiences is the ideal way to go about it. Here's why:

- **Promotes empathy and connection.** Sharing your experiences allows you to connect with your children personally. It lets them know you consider them equals because you demonstrate vulnerability and authenticity.

- **Encourages self-reflection.** Instead of prescribing solutions, sharing wisdom encourages your children to reflect on their own situation and draw their own conclusions. Hearing about your experiences may give them a different point of view and help them make informed decisions or navigate their challenges more effectively.

- **Respect autonomy.** Offering advice can sometimes come across as imposing your views or solutions onto your children, which may not always be welcome or appropriate. Sharing experiences, on the other hand, respects their autonomy and allows them to infer the right solutions based on your story.

- **Promotes active listening.** Essentially, your child will listen to you actively if you are saying something they are interested in. When you subtly share your experiences or wisdom, the focus is on the narrative being shared rather than on the message conveyed. This encourages them to fully absorb and reflect without feeling pressured to respond or act immediately on the solution.

- **Encourages a learning mindset.** Hearing about your experiences and wisdom can be a valuable learning opportunity for your children. It opens up new perspectives, broadens their understanding of different situations, and helps them consider alternative approaches to their own challenges.

- **Breaks down walls.** Young adults are more receptive to learning from others' experiences than receiving unsolicited advice. Sharing experiences in a non-preachy manner can help break down walls and create a more supportive and collaborative atmosphere.

How to Share Your Wisdom

There is a very thin line between wisdom-sharing and giving advice. Even while sharing a story, it is possible to make it sound like you're offering advice. Here are a few tips to avoid crossing this line:

- Start by being open and authentic about your own experiences. Share genuine and honest stories from your life, including successes and failures. Don't think of it as moralizing. This can help your children see you as relatable and encourage them to open up about their experiences.

- Look for appropriate opportunities to share your experiences when your children seem open and receptive. Avoid forcing the conversation or sharing too much at once, as this can be overwhelming. Instead, wait for natural openings in conversation or moments when they express interest in a particular topic.

- Avoid presenting a perfect or idealized version of yourself, as this can create barriers to a genuine connection. Don't exaggerate, either. Narrate the story exactly as you remember it.

- Share your experiences through storytelling, using real-life anecdotes to illustrate essential lessons or values. However, focus on the story instead of the lessons. They should not think you are using your experiences to offer advice. Don't underestimate them, either. Being inauthentic is easily spotted.

- Invite your children to engage in a dialogue about your experiences by asking open-ended questions and actively listening to their responses. For instance, "How did you find the experience?" or "What did you like about it?" Encourage them to share their own thoughts, feelings, and perspectives and be receptive to their input. Creating a two-way exchange of ideas about the same experience can strengthen your bond.

- Avoid the temptation to lecture or impose your views on them if they don't understand what you are trying to convey. Instead, offer your experiences as a source of guidance and wisdom. They will draw their own conclusions, which may be different from yours. Let them be. Trust that they will learn and grow from their own experiences, just as you have from yours.

- Be subtle while including the values and principles that underpin your experiences. Indirectly help them see how those values have guided you through life's challenges and empowered you to live with purpose and meaning. In fact, you should wait for them to bring their inferences into the limelight before having a deeper conversation.

- For example, instead of saying something like confidence helped you achieve your goals, attach the principal trait to the story by saying that you achieved your goals with confidence.

To help you draw a more vivid line between sharing wisdom and offering advice, consider this: Your child shared their college experience of losing a football game and continuously blames other teammates for the defeat. How can you make them accept responsibility and share the blame instead of laying it?

If you directly point out, "It's not right to blame others. You must have done something wrong too," they will not accept your view and may even stop talking to you. Instead, share your experience of a football game when you tried to find faults with everyone but later realized you were also to blame.

Narrate it as a connecting experience where your child feels you're trying to empathize and make them feel good about the loss. But when they think about it later, they may realize their mistake. It can be any team game or activity related to their experience, not necessarily the same sport.

Avoid Criticism

Criticism can be beneficial if taken the right way. It can pinpoint problems you never knew you had. It helps you gain a fresh perspective and discover new things about yourself. It gives you the much-needed push to achieve all your goals. However, your adult children may not see things this way.

They may feel you're needlessly criticizing them when all you're trying to do is help them be the best versions of themselves. They are already stressed about their college, work, friendships, and other relationships. By criticizing them, you are adding to their burden. Additionally, it doesn't take long for you to make a habit of criticizing as you start pointing out their every mistake. Let's take a closer look at why you should avoid criticism:

Negative Impact on Self-Esteem

Harsh criticism can damage your children's self-esteem and confidence, especially during their young adult years. Constant criticism without acknowledgment of positive aspects can demotivate them to the point of depression.

Resistance to Feedback

Excessive criticism can make them defensive and resistant to feedback, blocking their ability to learn and grow. When criticism is seen as unfair or unwarranted, it may cause them to dismiss valuable information.

Deterioration of Relationships

Continuous criticism, particularly when delivered without empathy or consideration for your children's feelings, can strain your relationship with them. It may lead to resentment and conflict, creating a negative atmosphere in your household.

Fear of Taking Risks

Children experiment with new things and take risks in their young adult years. Fear of being criticized can discourage them from taking even the most negligible risks. You may think it will keep your child safe from harm, but it does the exact opposite. This fear of failure can stifle creativity and innovation, as they may opt for safe choices to avoid potential criticism.

Impact on Mental Health

Persistent criticism can contribute to stress, anxiety, and even depression. Constant negative feedback can erode mental well-being and lead to burnout. They say even enduring, ageless trees cannot survive the continuous lashings of negativity. Your children, though adults, are still young.

Ineffectiveness of Communication

Criticism delivered without tact or diplomacy may not effectively convey the intended message. It can lead to misunderstandings, defensiveness, and escalate conflicts rather than begin a constructive dialogue.

Undermining Confidence and Initiative

It can bring down your children's confidence in their abilities and reduce their drive to take the initiative. Instead of feeling empowered to take action, they may become hesitant and passive, fearing further criticism.

Loss of Motivation

When criticism outweighs positive reinforcement, your children may lose motivation and enthusiasm for their work or studies. Without recognition for their efforts and achievements, they may question the value of their contributions.

Essentially, criticism is a harsher form of giving advice. You should avoid it as much as you can. But then, what should you do when you want your children to learn from their mistakes and be the best versions of themselves? Go with the storytelling technique discussed in the previous section, or give constructive feedback.

Tips to Give Constructive Feedback

- **Start with a positive note.** Begin by highlighting something your children did well or achieved. This sets a positive tone for the conversation and helps them feel valued and open to feedback.

- **Be specific and descriptive.** Focus on the particular behavior or outcome you want to address. Use concrete examples to illustrate your points, making them easier to understand.

- **Frame your feedback as observations and suggestions rather than criticism.** Use neutral language and avoid blaming or attacking their character.

- **Use the "Feedback Sandwich" approach.** Sandwich constructive criticism between positive feedbacks. Start with praise, provide areas for improvement, and end with a few motivational sentences or encouragement.

- **Provide feedback as soon as possible after the observed behavior or event.** This ensures that the details are fresh in your children's minds, making the feedback more relevant and impactful.

- **Focus on their behavior, not their personality.** Separate your children from their actions. Instead of judging their character, address specific behavioral traits that can be modified or improved.

- **Consider their feelings and perspectives.** Show empathy and respect for their efforts and intentions, even if the outcome isn't ideal.

- **Communicate your feedback clearly and straightforwardly.** Avoid vague or ambiguous language. Construct it in your mind before saying it out loud.

- **Invite your children to share their perspectives and ideas for improvement.** This will not only give them an opportunity to find solutions on their own but also show them you value their opinions.

- **Focus on solutions and growth soon after you have given the feedback.** Give advice only if they ask for it. If they don't, try the storytelling technique or direct them to useful resources where they can find the answers. Let them chart their own path in addressing the feedback and growing into the adults they were meant to be.

- **Check in with them periodically.** This is to see how they're progressing and offer additional support or guidance as needed. Don't be nagging or intrusive.

Here's an example you can refer to for giving constructive feedback to your children:

Positive note:
You've been doing excellent work in managing your responsibilities. Your dedication to your studies and your commitment to your part-time job is admirable.

Specific feedback:

However, you've been staying up very late recently, and it seems to be affecting your energy levels during the day. Yesterday, you mentioned feeling tired and overwhelmed while discussing your coursework.

Suggestion for improvement:

Establishing a consistent sleep schedule could benefit you. Perhaps you could create a bedtime routine that helps you wind down earlier and ensures you get enough rest each night. You can try minimizing screen time before bed and incorporating relaxation techniques like reading or listening to music."

Encouragement:

Prioritizing your sleep will improve your energy levels and concentration and also help your overall well-being and performance. You're capable of making positive changes in your life all on your own but don't hesitate to reach out if you ever need any help.

CHAPTER 2:

Establishing Boundaries with Love and Respect

—❖—

Navigating independence is a crucial aspect of your child's journey into adulthood. In this chapter, you will learn to set emotional and financial boundaries to create an environment where your child can thrive independently while still having a safety net of support. Whether it's about gradually introducing financial responsibilities, instilling values of responsibility, or keeping the lines of communication open, this chapter outlines the skills and mindset needed for a harmonious transition into adulthood.

Despite your young adult being around 18–25, they still might need your guidance and support to establish boundaries and to be independent.

When striving for independence, the first element to work on is how to establish boundaries. To define boundaries effectively, all you need to do is to communicate with transparency. For example, you can begin open conversations with your young adult about expectations to create a platform for mutual understanding. In discussions like these, you can express your needs, desires, and concerns, creating a cooperative approach to their independence. Through open communication, you can share your aspirations and apprehensions, paving the way for shared goals and a balanced dynamic between your and their autonomy and the support needed by both of you.

Encouraging Open Conversations

Understanding Expectations

Take the time to understand expectations. Discussing aspirations, concerns, and goals creates a foundation for mutual understanding, laying the groundwork for a balance between independence and support.

Creating a Platform for Dialogue

Encourage an environment where open communication is welcomed, ensuring that everyone feels comfortable expressing their thoughts and feelings and increasing trust. It will also help everyone understand expectations, making the journey toward independence collaborative.

Addressing Concerns

You can use conversations to address any concerns or uncertainties about the transition to independence. As you speak your mind, let your young adult express their concerns. Having discussions like these makes cooperation and supporting each other much more straightforward.

Setting Goals

Just like you conveyed your concerns and listened, encourage them to share their goals with you. For example, you can discuss the living arrangements you made when starting an independent life or share personal development objectives. After sharing these goals, ask them about their goals and aspirations. It creates a common ground where everyone is invested in the process, promoting teamwork.

Financial Responsibilities

Although you will be reading about these responsibilities in the next chapter, here are some basics your young adult should know when transitioning into adulthood:

- Invest time to teach the fundamental concepts of budgeting, saving, and responsible spending. Making informed spending decisions becomes much easier when your young adult has the necessary knowledge about budgeting, saving, and similar financial responsibilities. This will be the first step in developing financial literacy and independence in your child. The more time you put into teaching financial basics, the better they become.

- Gradually try to assign certain financial responsibilities like managing a personal budget or giving them money to manage specific expenses like paying the monthly internet bill. With this hands-on experience, their practical skills will improve and will increase a sense of accountability.

As managing finances is a key step toward independence, always encourage a learning mindset.

Instilling Values of Responsibility

Assigning Household Chores

Doing household chores is an excellent way for your young adult to understand and soak in the values of the responsibility of running a home. Specific tasks like knowing which day the trash is collected, how to clean gutters, where to pay utilities, and when are some chores they can take over to prepare for their own homes.

Remember that engaging in household chores goes beyond mere task completion. They teach practical life skills, from basic home maintenance to time management.

Encouraging Part-Time Jobs

Encourage your child to explore part-time employment opportunities. Besides earning some extra cash, a part-time job introduces them to the professional world, helping them develop interpersonal skills, improve their time management, and begin to understand workplace dynamics.

Besides bringing your youngster closer to financial independence, part-time jobs also teach essential money management skills. You can advise your young adult to spend their income wisely by making a budget or saving for something special. The idea here is to inspire them to make responsible financial decisions. The part-time job experience will also make it easier for them to explore hidden interests and strengths, improving personal and professional growth.

Engaging in both household chores and part-time employment creates a robust work ethic. When your youngster juggles personal responsibilities with work commitments, it teaches them how to be diligent, reliable, and persevere in demanding situations. When practiced correctly, the qualities and skills learned can become integral to their character, shaping the approach to challenges and opportunities in life.

While assigning them responsibilities is always a proactive step, never overemphasize or force them. As a parent, you need to make sure to support and guide them through this crucial phase.

Encouraging Emotional Resilience

Empowering Decision-Making

A crucial aspect of achieving independence is developing emotional resilience. Give your young adult the space to make decisions independently. This autonomy builds confidence and sharpens their decision-making skills. During their journey, teach them to trust their inner self and realize that mistakes are a natural part of any learning process.

Balancing Independence With Guidance

Tell your young adult that guidance is always available whenever they need it. You can monitor their activities and engagements and be ready to jump in to offer advice when needed, especially when you might see an emotional impact. This balance between making independent decisions and seeking guidance creates a supportive environment where they can learn from their experiences and continue to grow their skills.

Likewise, explain that setbacks are opportunities for growth. Whenever your young adult encounters challenges and bounces back from adversity, it shapes their character, teaching them about perseverance and self-discovery. Along the way, you need to create a framework where mistakes are viewed as stepping stones rather than failures. This mindset shift allows them to make decisions with a sense of curiosity and courage while keeping emotional influences at bay.

Managing Emotions

Part of emotional resilience is acknowledging and managing emotions. Explain that it's okay to feel a range of emotions. Although this emotional surge can temporarily decrease their decision-making skills, it can help develop a deeper understanding of the inner self. Self-awareness is a powerful tool in navigating life's challenges.

Encouraging a Positive Mindset

Promote a positive mindset, focusing on solutions rather than dwelling on problems. This proactive approach empowers young adults to tackle challenges with optimism and creativity, surrounding them with a support system that encourages a positive outlook on life and reinforces emotional resilience.

Celebrating Achievements

Always acknowledge and celebrate achievements, no matter how small. Recognizing these successes builds a positive self-image and boosts the ability to overcome obstacles. These celebrations act as reminders of the capabilities your child has developed and make them emotionally stable.

Respecting Privacy

Understanding Boundaries

The first thing to do is focus on respecting your child's privacy. Everyone has different personal space and information comfort levels, so recognizing and understanding these limits can become a minefield. As long as your communication with your young adult is characterized by trust, your relationship will be in good shape.

Communication and Consent

Take your young adult aside to discuss privacy expectations. Ask them about their expectations and encourage them to be honest and expressive. Discuss what areas are considered private and ensure consent before entering personal spaces.

Balancing Independence and Respect

While striving for independence, it's essential to strike a balance between individual freedom and respecting the privacy of others. Remind them about using shared spaces considerately. Cultivating this awareness of others' boundaries promotes mutual respect and makes it easier for everyone to openly discuss boundaries.

Create an atmosphere of comfort and security when discussing sensitive issues, such as expressing their need for privacy. The discussions won't be fruitful if they fear judgment from parents or peers. Emphasize communicating openly about what they think of having a personal space and why they might need it.

Respecting Digital Boundaries

In this digital age, respecting privacy extends to online spaces. Educate them on the drawbacks of sharing personal information and the implications of accessing others' devices without permission.

When teaching about privacy, remember that individual needs may vary. Some may be more private about personal matters, while others may be comfortable with a more communal approach. Depending on your child's comfort level, it can take an hour to several days to define boundaries and learn about respecting privacy.

Being Available for Support

Understanding Emotional Needs

Being available for support starts with understanding the emotional needs of your young adult. Pay attention to verbal and nonverbal cues that indicate they may be facing challenges or experiencing stress. When you know what emotional state they are in, it becomes easier to offer meaningful support.

Providing Practical Help

Being available for support is not just about emotional reassurance; it also involves practical assistance. Whether assisting with tasks, providing resources, or offering guidance, always lend a helping hand when requested. Taking concrete actions demonstrates your commitment to being a reliable and supportive presence.

Maintaining an Open Line of Communication

Personal responsibilities, workload, or family dynamics can sometimes weaken communication with your young adult. That's when you have to step up your communication game. For example, you can't establish boundaries or know about their aspirations unless they are comfortable communicating without holding back.

No matter how busy your schedule is, make it a routine to take some time out for your soon-to-be independent child and discuss their day or any concerns they have worrying them. However, remember to keep the conversations casual so they feel comfortable sharing. During your conversations, affirm that you are available for discussions or support whenever needed. Make it known that you are actively listening, willing to guide, or simply be a sounding board. It will encourage your young adult to reach out without hesitation. Make sure your body language, tone, and responses convey approachability, not parental authority. They won't express themselves if they don't see you as approachable.

Furthermore, you recognize and respect that your young adult may have a different communication style. Some prefer direct and verbal communication, while others may express themselves more comfortably through writing or other forms. Be adaptable to these different styles so that communication remains open and effective. While encouraging open communication, it's essential to respect the boundaries. Be mindful of the timing and context of your conversations, ensuring that discussions are welcomed and appropriate. This practice creates a healthy exchange of thoughts and feelings without intruding on personal boundaries.

Establishing Boundaries With Love and Respect

Empathy is a fundamental pillar of healthy relationships, particularly when guiding young adults. It's more than just understanding someone's feelings; it's about creating an environment where everyone feels valued and supported.

Whether it's lending an ear or pouring your heart out, authentic communication is the key. So, when you're teaching and talking about empathy, the first step is to encourage listening without interrupting or formulating responses. Another practical way is to practice giving your full attention, especially when your young adult is expressing their thoughts or feelings. Make eye contact, nod in acknowledgment, and avoid interrupting. After doing this a few times, you can explain to them the reason behind this practice and how it can promote empathy.

A mature, empathetic person can see things from another person's perspective, understand their emotions, and acknowledge their experiences. These are the lessons that need to be taught. Discuss with your child how they would approach a certain situation if they were in the same place; consider what decisions could be beneficial and what might be harmful.

Furthermore, your young adult needs to understand the importance of emotional validation. Encourage them to use phrases like "I can see why you might feel that way" or "Your feelings are valid" when they need to be empathetic and to create a safe space for open communication.

Although discussing different perspectives, listening, and validating emotions are part of empathy, your goal is to create a culture in your young adult that values understanding and compassion. The key is to encourage empathy as a shared value. Share stories that highlight empathy, celebrate instances of understanding, and be clear that everyone's feelings and experiences are valid and respected.

After establishing a foundation, take it up a notch and encourage your young adult to pay attention to their posture and facial expressions when having empathetic conversations. Explain to them that open body language, eye contact while talking, and facial expressions convey warmth and understanding. Genuine empathy is often reflected in actions that demonstrate care and consideration for others' feelings.

When you create an environment of understanding, practice empathy, and value the emotions of people around you, the young adult you want to become independent will naturally learn from the experience.

Whether in a household or a workplace, each person is unique with their own set of strengths, weaknesses, and dreams. As you continue to work with your young adult, instill the value of recognizing and celebrating these differences. Just like you embrace and appreciate the distinct qualities of those in your life, encourage your young adult and their friends to express their individuality, allowing everyone to follow their aspirations and contribute their talents to the collective dynamic.

As you know, life is dynamic and constantly evolving. To make sure your young adult can handle the heat, encourage them to be adaptable. As they navigate through life's twists and turns, guide them to be open-minded and flexible.

Teaching Conflict Resolution Skills

Conflict is inevitable in any relationship, but how your young adult approaches and resolves it can make a significant difference. Teaching conflict resolution skills enables them to navigate disagreements constructively. These skills include active listening, expressing feelings assertively yet respectfully, and working collaboratively toward solutions.

Nurturing Self-Care Practices

In the journey to become independent, self-care practices are crucial for sustaining a healthy body and mind. Besides eating a balanced diet, sleeping properly and enough, and exercising, do things that bring you joy, relaxation, and fulfillment. Encourage others to do the same.

Setting Personal Goals

Establishing personal goals is an excellent way to cultivate self-growth and fulfillment. You can help them identify their aspirations, both short-term and long-term, and actively work toward them. You can even share your personal goals and encourage your young adult to do the same in an environment where everyone is supported. Setting and achieving personal goals brings a sense of accomplishment and makes life fulfilling and purposeful.

As you help your child establish boundaries, teach them to self-reflect. It's an examination of the boundaries they put in place. Encourage them to consider whether their boundaries align with their values and if they need adjustment based on changing circumstances.

Furthermore, explain to your young adult that boundaries are sometimes negotiable and subject to compromise. When conflicts arise, they have to approach them with an open mind and a willingness to find a middle ground. This may involve adjusting the boundaries to accommodate others. However, no one's needs should be compromised when adjusting these boundaries.

When boundaries are poorly maintained, there can be consequences. For example, if a boundary is consistently ignored, the consequence might involve a reduction in shared responsibilities. Teach them that setting poor boundaries and avoiding shared responsibilities only breaks trust and collaboration in any relationship.

Likewise, when anyone sets a boundary, time and space are often needed to adjust. Change doesn't happen overnight, especially when it involves reshaping how the family interacts. Teach your young adult that not everyone will immediately grasp or accept the new boundaries that are implemented. Encountering some resistance or pushback is inevitable, and that's okay.

There might be moments when things don't go as smoothly as hoped, and that's when patience really comes into play. Instead of getting frustrated, instill the idea that progress takes time. Remember, Rome wasn't built in a day, and neither are strong family bonds with clear boundaries. So, take it one step at a time, be kind to yourself and others, and trust that with patience, things will gradually fall into place.

Seek Professional Guidance

During the path to establishing and setting boundaries, progress might be slow. It happens due to things like excessive academic pressure, having low self-esteem, and even suffering from a mental health condition. When it comes to assisting your young adult in setting boundaries, seeking professional guidance can work like magic as they have the right expertise to guide you through the process. Professionals, like therapists and counselors, are trained to offer an impartial perspective uninfluenced by familial biases. They possess the knowledge and skills to navigate complex family dynamics and can provide strategies suited to specific circumstances. Depending on the unique circumstances, a therapist will thoroughly evaluate and suggest therapy for your child or the whole family. These therapies are like activities targeted to identify, enhance, and address problems that can come in the way of progress. For example, when it comes to establishing boundaries, the professional can suggest a therapy that furnishes a safe environment conducive to open communication, enabling everyone to express themselves freely. Furthermore, boundary issues stem from underlying conflicts or past traumas, which professionals can help identify and address. Teaching effective communication techniques and offering ongoing support can help you establish and maintain healthy boundaries and develop solid relationships.

CHAPTER 3:

Fostering Independence and Responsibility

—❖—

As your teen matures into a young adult, their parenting requirements will also have to grow to equip them with the life skills they'll need to succeed beyond their academic performance. In reading this chapter, you'll learn how to empower your young adult with the tools, advice, and techniques to develop financial literacy, practice self-care, and solve their problems effectively and independently. From budgeting and investing to stress management and decision-making, they will feel independent while trusting that your advice and support are there as a safety net. Encouraging your child to rely on themselves throughout their teen years will better equip them to handle their responsibilities and focus on their well-being as a young adult. Eventually, they will grow into a resilient and driven adult.

Teaching Your Young Adult Financial Skills

Teaching your young adult how money works and sound financial habits can set them up for sound financial security. Not all schools offer personal finance courses, which means they might not learn these skills at all if they don't learn them from you. Understanding how to budget, save, invest, manage their debts, and plan their taxes will ensure that your grown-up child develops a healthy relationship with money. They'll be able to make smart financial decisions as they move along the next phases of life.

When they go to college, your young adult will be responsible for earning and managing an income, as well as their academics, home management, and healthcare. Many college students make the life-altering mistake of rushing to set up a credit card, only to find themselves drowning in debt a few months later. Be sure to teach your children early about the debt trap and other pitfalls of easy finance that are glibly advertised. Talk to them about the alternatives and gradually give them more control over their money. They'll learn best when they do it themselves.

Practicing money management when they have fewer responsibilities is an equally valuable experience with fewer consequences. Talk about money openly to help them feel more comfortable around the subject. Growing up in a household where finances are kept secret can lead to unhealthy relationships with finances and cause your young adult to shy away from asking you questions or discussing their financial troubles with you.

Budgeting and Saving

- **Make saving money a habit.** Start by explaining how saving a portion of their money will ensure they have enough to fund unexpected needs, future expenses, and emergencies. Highlight the fact that unanticipated events happen all the time. They might crash their car, lose their job and not find another one right away, damage their phone, or have an emergency. Introduce savings apps and automatic transfers. Brainstorm a reasonable saving percentage to put away each month.

- **Teach them about the difference between wants and needs.** Encourage them to think about whether they need something or simply want it before completing a transaction. Do they *need* to buy this backpack? If their current one is still in good shape, then they *want* a new one. If it's no longer good to use, then they *need* a new one. Do they *want* to go out with their friends or do they *need* it to boost their mental or emotional health? Remember that each person's needs are different, so make sure to put that into perspective when discussing budgeting with your young adult. Instill concepts like delayed gratification and mindful spending. Teach them to spend 50% of their income on their needs, 30% on their wants, and save the remaining amount.

- **Set up a tracking system.** This system is not for you to track their savings but for them to understand the impact of spending or saving money. Get them to open a savings bank account and use online banking tools to track their spending. Or they could also use something as simple as an envelope system. When they track their spending and see the impact on their bank account in real time, they'll feel more responsible.

- **Create a financial plan.** Work with them to set reasonable financial goals. Create a savings strategy that isn't too strict that it causes stress and isn't so lenient that they are unable to achieve their goals. Brainstorm both short-term and long-term goals, such as buying a new phone, car, or house, paying off their tuition, or saving up for retirement. Ask them what changes they can make to manage their finances to achieve these goals and what they need to do, career-wise, to get there.

Investing

- **Familiarize them with the basics.** Teach your young adults the importance of investments in creating passive income, building wealth, and achieving long-term financial goals. Discuss key concepts and terms, such as stocks, bonds, ETFs, and mutual funds, and explain what each means, how they work, and their pros and cons.

- **Give them examples of popular companies.** Select popular companies that are familiar to them to make the concepts more relatable. Discuss these companies' business models, revenue streams, and financial performance. Explain how investors benefit when the companies they have invested in are performing well. Browse through forecasts together to give your young adult a better understanding of how investors choose which companies to invest in, as well as the industries and trends they select based on their potential and performance.

- **Explain the importance of portfolio diversification.** One of the greatest mistakes a novice investor can make is failing to diversify their investments. Making diverse investments doesn't only require you to invest in different companies but also different industries, geographic locations, and classes. This can reduce volatility and risk, as individual stocks are fluctuant by nature.

- **Teach them to buy and hold.** One of the essential things to do before investing is to develop patience and discipline. The investment market is known for its volatility, and success usually comes in the long term. This is why you should teach them the principle of "buy and hold." They should choose quality companies to invest in and then hold their investments for the long term to minimize transaction costs and increase their investment returns over time.

Debt Management

- **Teach them to buy what they can afford.** You wouldn't use your credit card to buy things you can afford. However, if you need to buy something that cash can't cover, make sure that you can afford to pay off in due time. Teach them to prioritize paying off their debt as soon as they earn income; otherwise, credit card bills will accumulate. You need to bring to their attention that they might be charged lower interest rates in some banks because they're students, but it doesn't mean that they should overspend.

- **Explain that budgeting is critical.** After you've created a budgeting plan that allows your young adult to know exactly where every dollar is spent, encourage them to stick to it. Budgeting money effectively is the key to avoiding getting into debt. If the budgeting plan is not working for them and they feel the need to borrow money frequently, it's obvious a rethink is needed. When creating a budgeting and spending plan, they should automatically deduct money that must be paid, such as bills, rent, and other expenses, and then see what they're going to do with the rest of the money.

- **Explain what paying off debt actually looks like.** Explain the concept of interest to your new adult. If they borrow $100 from the bank, they might repay it as $120. The interest could be less or lower, depending on the bank. $20 might not seem like a big deal. However, if they borrow an additional $50, they'll pay an extra $10, and if they make another purchase at $200, they'll pay $40 interest. Instead of paying a total of $350, they'll end up having to repay $420 to the bank if the interest rate is 20%. That's $70 that you could've put toward their savings or another short-term goal.

- **Make sure they understand the repercussions of ignoring debts.** If a debt isn't paid on time, their credit score will go down, making it hard to get a mortgage to buy a house, an auto loan to purchase a car, or access any other type of credit later on. If they were lucky enough to access credit, then they would be charged a higher interest rate.

Taxes

- **Teach them about income and taxes.** Explain to them the different types of income they can earn, such as allowances, wages, and income from investments. Ensure they understand the difference between taxable and non-taxable income and know the tax brackets and progressive taxation. It helps to involve them in the process when you're calculating your taxes because it can help them grasp the concept more effectively. Explain how taxes are calculated based on each person's income levels, exemptions, credits, and deductions.

- **Explain the different tax forms and documentation.** Familiarize them with common tax forms and explain what each is used for. You should also highlight the importance of keeping track of income and expenses. Explain that receipts and bank statements are crucial when filing for taxes, and give them tips on keeping these documents organized.

- **Teach them to manage their finances.** Emphasize the significance of budgeting, tracking their spending, investing, and setting financial goals regarding taxes. Explain the consequences of tax noncompliance and maintaining ethical behaviors when it comes to finances. Give them tips on how to plan their taxes, such as maximizing credits and deductions.

Encouraging Self-Care and Well-Being

As a parent, you're probably losing your mind trying to do your best at work to provide for your family, including maintaining your home and ensuring your family has food on the table. You're likely trying to find the perfect balance between all these pressures and keeping an eye on your children's academics and personal lives. If anyone needs to practice self-care and look out for their overall well-being, you probably think it's you.

Everyone should practice self-care and focus on their well-being because no one has it easy. Your young adult probably faces great stress and pressure as they try to balance college with their jobs while maintaining a healthy social life. There's pressure at home from family members and pressure from social media. They have full-day schedules at college, study, do assignments, extracurricular activities, socialize, and work. They do that while navigating a period of self-discovery and trying to understand who they are and what they want in life.

Young adults learn what it means to be truly independent for the first time. They start working full-time jobs and become fully financially responsible while exploring the realm of serious romantic relationships, marriage, losing and making new friends, and other troubles.

Children, too, face stress and pressure. An eight-year-old has never been in third grade before. Being there, they have to adapt to the increased academic load while doing a sport or other extracurricular activities and potentially facing issues with their peers. Teens are subject to peer pressure and are torn between who they want to be and who they need to be to fit in.

The takeaway is that regardless of how old they are, everyone needs self-care for their overall well-being. Everyone is living life for the first time. Your young adult has never experienced this phase of their life before and is therefore still learning to navigate the challenges it throws at them, just as this might be your first time raising a young adult, and you are reading this book for advice on how to make their life easier or raise them right. Self-care is essential for everyone because it helps alleviate stress, prevent depression, and help with grounding and coping using healthy methods.

Mental and Emotional Health

- **Teach them that asking for help is a sign of strength, not weakness.** You want your children, no matter how old they grow, to be able to discuss their problems and seek help whenever they need it. They need to understand that reaching out for help doesn't make them any less capable or resilient. Ask their opinions in situations you find challenging, talk about your problems with them, and encourage them to share theirs. Explain the importance of reaching out for support without making them feel forced to share.

- **A balanced lifestyle is the key to a balanced life.** Explain that healthy habits are as important for mental health as they are for the body, such as eating a nutritious diet, exercising regularly, and getting enough sleep every night. As they navigate this new phase of their lives, young adults often forget to look out for their own needs.

- **Remind them to set achievable goals.** Young adults may often feel the need to do and achieve more. They fear that they're growing up too fast and that it's now or never that they build a bright future for themselves. While it's true that one's young adult years are filled with potentially life-shaping opportunities, you need to remind them that they still have their entire lives ahead of them. While setting lofty goals can be a great motivator, it can also lead to unnecessary pressure and disappointments.

- **When in doubt, remind them of their capabilities.** Everyone needs to hear words of encouragement from time to time. Just because your child is now all grown up doesn't mean you should stop reassuring them and giving them words of affirmation. Remind them that you're proud of everything they're doing.

- **Help them develop healthy coping mechanisms.** Encourage them to try different therapeutic activities, such as music, art, journaling, yoga, mindfulness, or therapy. Explain that there's nothing wrong with seeking professional help if needed, and ensure they surround themselves with a healthy support network. Highlight the importance of building positive relationships and connecting with uplifting people.

Other tips:

- Check in regularly with your young adult and make sure you create a safe space where they know they're never too old to reach out to you and feel encouraged to share their thoughts and feelings.

- Suggest that you spend quality time with them and do activities that help you bond and connect with them on a deeper level.

- Show interest in their hobbies and passions. This will encourage them to share their life's updates with you.

- Regularly reassure them that you're available and willing to support them whenever they ask.

- Discuss the negative impact of stress and overwhelm. Remind them to take breaks when needed.

- Respect their need for independence. Find the balance between respecting their need for autonomy and maintaining open lines of communication.

- Encourage them to partake in self-care practices and guide them toward managing stress effectively.

Physical Health

Regular Exercise

- **Ask your young adult whether they've been taking care of their physical health.** Exercise, fitness, and physical well-being are generally very sensitive topics to discuss with anyone. You want to make sure that your young adult is getting adequate regular exercise without making them feel like you're being too critical or controlling. You can mention a new type of exercise you're interested in and ask them to join you. You can explain that working out together is a great way to bond while encouraging each other to stay active. You'll both benefit by dedicating as little as 30 minutes of your day to any form of exercise you like, such as yoga, Pilates, running, or walking, as exercise can significantly reduce stress, build strength, enhance focus and energy, and improve mood.

- **Suggest that you engage in activities that they're interested in.** If they mention they're interested in a certain sport, suggest you join them. If you can't, you can ask if you can go watch them if they don't mind. Showing interest in their exercise choices can encourage them to keep active.

- **Develop a healthy mindset toward exercise.** Most importantly, as a family, you shouldn't be solely focused on the impact of exercise, or the lack thereof, on physical appearance. Exercise should be encouraged because it's enjoyable, promotes personal growth, and offers a wide array of physical and mental health benefits.

- **Celebrate their achievements.** Show interest in their sport and celebrate their progress, milestones, and achievements. If they haven't found a form of exercise that they like yet, encourage them to explore different activities until they find something that resonates with them without making them feel forced to exercise.

Adequate Sleep

- **Discuss the importance of sleep.** As they try to maintain a balance between all their new-found responsibilities, young adults may barely make enough time for sleep. If your young adult is open to discussing their sleep habits with you, mention that adequate sleep every night is crucial for their ability to reduce overwhelm and enhance their daily functions. While they might think that they can get more things done by reducing the number of hours they sleep every night, an unhealthy sleep schedule can reduce their productivity in the long run. Getting enough sleep can improve focus and cognitive function, enhance physical and emotional health, and lead to professional and academic achievement. Poor sleep patterns can lead to severe mood swings, irritability, emotional instability, poor emotional health, a lack of focus, and a negative impact on academic performance.

- **Explore the reasons behind poor sleep patterns.** Encourage them to find out why they might struggle with insufficient sleep or a delayed sleep schedule. Anxiety, overwhelm, stress, and overthinking can interfere with the ability to sleep well. They might need a better sleep environment or struggle with time management and barely have time to sleep. The problem might be that they engage in stimulating activities before bedtime, drink too much caffeine, excessively use electronics, or suffer from mental health or sleep conditions. Explain that understanding the causes is the key to finding solutions.

- **Help them develop good sleep hygiene.** If they're willing to accept advice, mention that they shouldn't engage in any stimulating activities before bed and encourage them to keep their electronic devices away at least 30 minutes prior. They can also journal or practice mindful techniques before bed to relax their mind and body. You could recommend that they limit caffeine consumption before bed and create a comfortable sleep environment (ideal room temperature at 65 °F, comfortable bedding, darkness, quiet, clutter-free).

- **Ask them to seek professional help if needed.** If they struggle with chronic sleep problems, ask them to consider consulting a doctor.

Eating a Balanced and Nutritious Diet

- **Know when and how to talk.** You should never sit your young adult down to have a talk about their eating habits. If you're concerned that they might not be eating nutritious meals and looking out for their health, make sure that they're open to discussing this topic to avoid giving them unsolicited advice. This topic is very sensitive, and approaching it in the wrong way can push your young adult away. You can simply start the conversation by saying, "I just want to make sure that you're eating well. I'm worried that you might not be looking out for your health or not have the time to make nutritious meals for yourself." Their response will dictate the rest of the conversation.

- **Share interesting recipe findings.** If they're open to discussing this topic, you can share interesting, healthy recipes you think they might like. Make sure that they're easy to prepare.

- **Cook nutritious meals for them.** You can prepare healthy meals for them and take them with you whenever you're visiting. They won't feel that you're imposing and will likely take it as a sign of love and care. You can also take healthy snack options, fruits, and vegetables with you. When healthy items are available, they will be more likely to reach for them whenever they need a quick snack.

- **Suggest you go grocery shopping together.** If they live nearby, suggest that you both go grocery shopping together as a way to make errands more enjoyable and use it as an opportunity to catch up. While you shouldn't tell them explicitly which types of products to buy, your choices will likely influence theirs.

Stress Management

- **Remind them to find the right balance between work, rest, and play.** Your young adult needs to dedicate enough time to their responsibilities, activities they enjoy, and rest. They need to have enough time to relax and mentally and physically recharge to avoid burning out. Remind them that there's nothing wrong with taking breaks and moving at a slow and steady pace.

- **Encourage them to plan their day.** If they mention that they're battling with time management, ask if they use to-do lists, calendars, and planning apps. As long as your communication is open, these are the things you can suggest without prescribing and being a "parent." Mention the importance of consistency when it comes to following new plans and staying on top of commitments. Remind them that positive changes are only difficult at first. Everything becomes easier with perseverance long enough that they become habits.

- **Encourage them to ask for help when needed.** Remind them that you'll always try your best to help them with personal or academic challenges or feelings of overwhelm and that you're willing to discuss any concerns or anxieties that they have.

- **Explain that stress is not necessarily a bad thing.** When it's excessive, stress can negatively impact one's mental, emotional, and physical health. However, healthy amounts of stress are needed to stay motivated.

- **Tackle problems effectively.** If they need advice regarding certain problems, mention that running away from problems only leads to more stress and pent-up emotions.

Developing Decision-Making and Problem-Solving Skills

- **Guide, but don't control.** Young adults make several life-altering decisions every day. Make it clear that you're open to offering them the guidance and support they need without judging their thoughts and feelings. Help them without micromanaging their decisions, and accept that they won't always take your advice into consideration. Remember that the consequences of their actions will teach them valuable lessons. Instead of saying, "I told you so," support them as they learn from their mistakes.

- **Determine the problems.** If your young adult is open to sharing their concerns with you, listen actively and avoid criticizing them to encourage them to keep open lines of communication. Make a conscious effort to understand them better. Encourage them to take responsibility for their problems, actively search for solutions, and own their decisions.

- **Brainstorm possible courses of action.** When your young adult shares a problem with you, encourage them to brainstorm as many solutions as possible, no matter how crazy they may seem. Creative thinking and exploring several perspectives widen their horizons. When they're done thinking of scenarios, guide them toward examining the potential pros and cons of each scenario. Have them evaluate the outcomes, as well as the thoughts and feelings that may be realized as a result of this option.

Now that you've read this chapter, you have a reasonable idea of how to raise an independent, capable, and confident young adult. You understand how to balance giving them autonomy and granting them independence while still looking out for their well-being and guiding their choices in different areas of their lives.

CHAPTER 4:

Supporting Educational and Career Paths

—❖—

Sometimes, it might feel like being a parent was easier when your children were young. At that age, they didn't know much about how life works, which meant you got to make all the major decisions for them. Even when you didn't see eye to eye, you knew you could always put your foot down if you had to keep them from hurting themselves or making bad choices.

Eventually, your child grows up. They'll want more autonomy, and you'll have no choice but to let them have it. At times, they'll listen to your advice, see the sense in it, and do what you suggest. Other times, they'll chart their own course. Your child doesn't always oppose you for the sake of it. It could be that they see things you can't from your perspective as an adult who grew up in different times from theirs.

As tempting as it is to get frustrated with your now young adult child, you have to let them have the space they need to make their decisions. If you want a child who grows up to be independent and confident, you have to step aside and let them make up their minds about the things that matter to them—especially regarding their education and career paths.

The sad truth is no one lives forever. It would be a shame and a burden for your young adult when you pass away, and they have to bear the consequences of the choices *you* made for them. This is why you should honor their agency. It will give them a sense of responsibility, too, rather than the tendency to blame everyone else when things go wrong because they never had the chance to decide for themselves.

Your young adult will ultimately find themselves in a career and spend years at work. It's only fair that they get to decide what careers interest them and the educational path they need to take to accomplish their dreams. The question is: What's your role in all this as a parent? You're there to offer support and share your experiences and knowledge on what you know about the careers your young adult is interested in. You're there to let them know the good, the bad, and the ugly (which are all relative) and help them select the best options—even if you disagree with it all, and more essentially, if you are asked.

In light of this role, this chapter is here to help you understand the educational and career challenges faced by young adults. You will find tips on creating a supportive environment for them and teaching them to deal with failures. With the knowledge contained in the next few pages, you can support your child in whatever way they need you to when it comes to their educational and career path. Keep reading.

Understanding the Challenges Faced by Young Adults

As parents, your constant concern for your children's well-being is understandable. The parent in you will always worry. But you're not the only one with things to worry about. Your young adults are often presented with a unique set of challenges. They feel pressured to "do well" academically, maintain a good image for college, and keep up with all the extracurricular activities. Looking back, you'll remember that navigating these expectations was also quite difficult for you.

Recognizing the Complexities and Uncertainties

Young adults today are confronted with a myriad of choices when it comes to their educational and career paths. From deciding between different fields of study to navigating the job market, the sheer range of options can be overwhelming. As children, they probably just wanted to be doctors, engineers, and astronauts, but now faced with the many options available, they might struggle with picking and sticking to one career path for a while. The rapidly evolving nature of industries and technology adds another layer of complexity, as what may be in demand today could become obsolete tomorrow. New styles and jobs are popping up daily as the world continues to evolve.

In addition, young adults are burdened by uncertainties about their future. It is a very confusing and scary time for them. They may feel unsure about which path is right for them or worry about making the wrong decision that could impact their lives in the long term. This uncertainty can lead to feelings of anxiety and stress, making the decision-making process even more challenging.

Societal Expectations and Peer Pressure

A child is born into a society and is groomed to fit in. One of the effects of this is that societal expectations play a significant role in shaping young adults' educational and career choices as the story of their lives unfolds. From a young age, they are bombarded with messages about the significance of pursuing prestigious careers or obtaining degrees from top-tier institutions. These expectations can create a sense of pressure to conform to certain standards of success, even if they do not fit with their own interests or passions.

What about peer pressure? Peer influence adds another layer of stress as young adults compare themselves to their friends or classmates who look like they have their lives figured out. This comparison will cause them to start feeling inadequate, leading to self-doubt and possibly depression. All this is due to the fear of falling behind or not measuring up to the perceived success of their mates.

You may not see it, but your young adult may also wrestle with their own aspirations and ambitions on the inside. They may feel torn between following their passions and interests versus pursuing a path that offers stability and financial security. As they try to balance these internal desires with external pressures, they might be plagued with tension and stress that may show up in bursts of frustration.

In times like these, your young adult needs empathy from you. You need an awareness of the multitude of factors influencing their decision-making processes. Acknowledging the complexities and pressures they encounter, parents can provide more meaningful support and guidance as their young adult children navigate their educational and career paths.

Educational Challenges Young Adults Face

For young adults, figuring out the educational dos and don'ts can feel like wandering in a fog. They're wrestling with big decisions: Which college or university to attend, what to major in, and how to handle the demands of academics. It's a lot to take in. As a parent, you need to create an environment where they feel comfortable discussing their interests, strengths, and dreams. Guide them through exploring different educational pathways—from traditional colleges to vocational programs or online courses. Help them understand the significance of following their passions rather than simply succumbing to outside influences or societal norms. Some educational challenges they face include:

- The constant pressure to succeed. Tests, projects, applications, and so on. Young adults have to balance all this with figuring out who they are.

- Finding the right path isn't like tying a shoelace or knotting a tie. As parents who were once young adults yourself, you should know a thing or two about how difficult this period in your life was. These days, young adults have so many choices—different colleges and different programs. What if they pick the wrong one? What if all that money goes to waste?

- They struggle to keep up with the times. The world is changing so fast; what they learn today might be outdated tomorrow. Are schools even keeping up? Will their skills still be relevant in a few years?

- Focusing too much on getting degrees can hold young people back from growing in other ways. While degrees are good, they're not the only way to succeed. Nowadays, employers want more than just degrees—they want people with practical skills and experience. If young adults only focus on getting degrees, they might miss chances to learn these skills. So what should they do?

- Another challenge is that many schools still use old-fashioned teaching plans, making it hard for young people to keep up with what employers need. Schools need to update their teaching methods to match what is required in the workplace, but until then, it is entirely up to young adults to figure out how to prepare themselves for future jobs.

Career Challenges Young Adults Face

Getting started on the journey of building a career is not something a young adult usually looks forward to. The many career paths available can leave them feeling overwhelmed at first. Still, it presents a lot of opportunities and possibilities to explore and discover what they are passionate about. As a parent, you need to make time for meaningful conversations about their career aspirations, what they value, and where they see themselves a few years from the present.

Rather than feeling pressured to make definitive decisions, guide them toward dipping their toes in various waters—internships, part-time gigs, volunteering, and so on, to get a feel for different industries and roles. Remind them that careers often take unexpected detours and that it's okay to embrace the twists and turns along the way. Some common challenges include the following:

- These days, a lot of people chase after instant gratification. Many want things immediately without having to wait or even do the required work. This makes young adults think about quick goals, like earning lots of money fast, instead of thinking about their future success. This way of thinking can make it hard for them to learn the skills and knowledge they'll need later on.

- Finding that first job can be difficult, especially when everyone talks about having "work experience." This can be frustrating to young adults, making them feel it's impossible to get a good job. However, encourage your young adult to take entry-level positions. They present a chance for young adults to learn new skills and grow. Even if the starting point seems small, entry-level jobs are like stepping stones leading to bigger and better things. So, tell them to jump in enthusiastically and make the most of it.

- It can be challenging for young adults to know how to manage everything, especially when they might not have much experience with bills and budgets. So, talk to them openly about money and help them create a plan for how to track income and expenses. This way, young adults can learn to be smart with their cash. You can also help them explore options for financial aid or part-time work to ease the burden.

- Competition in the job market is fierce, with everyone vying for a coveted spot. Even armed with a degree, there's no guarantee of landing a job that pays well and utilizes their hard-earned skills. This period of their lives will likely affect their mental health as they try to find their footing in the world. Encourage them to stay positive and determined as they navigate the twists and turns of the job search. Remind them they are tougher than they think. It will only be a matter of time, and all their hard work will pay off.

How to Foster a Supportive Environment for Your Young Adult

While the transition from childhood to young adulthood might seem stress-free, it often comes with significant challenges for young individuals. This is where you come in. As a parent, you play an important role in helping them navigate this overwhelming period of their lives. Your young adults need your understanding and support as a foundation upon which they build a solid and successful future. Here are some key strategies to create a supportive environment for them to thrive on:

- **Start by creating a safe space.** There are certain ways you can create an environment where your young adult feels secure in expressing their interests, passions, and strengths. This involves creating an atmosphere of trust and understanding within the family setting—where conversations are held non-judgmentally and differing viewpoints are welcomed and respected. Encourage your young adult to share their thoughts and aspirations freely, assuring them that their feelings and opinions are valued.

- **Give them room to speak.** You start to win the battle when your children come to you about anything that bothers them. Promoting open communication lays the foundation for your young adult to explore various avenues without fear of criticism or condemnation. Find out about their interests, and encourage them even if they seem unconventional or divergent from your expectations. Make them understand how important it is to have honest and transparent conversations where both parties feel heard and understood.

- **The world is full of options.** Please understand that there is no "one-size-fits-all" approach to education and career choices. The world is indeed full of a diverse array of options to consider. Your young adult might excel in a traditional academic setting, pursuing a degree in a field that ignites their curiosity. Alternatively, vocational training could be a fantastic avenue, equipping them with valuable technical skills for in-demand careers. For the entrepreneurial spirit, starting a venture they're passionate about could be incredibly rewarding. Don't let their creativity go to waste. Tell them how valuable self-discovery and experimentation are, and allow them to pursue paths that align with their passions and aspirations rather than conform to societal expectations or predefined norms.

- **Teach them about self-reflection.** You can guide them through the process of self-reflection and help them discover their interests, strengths, and core values. Encourage them to start journaling, which can be incredibly beneficial. Journaling provides a space to explore their thoughts and feelings, free from external judgment. Self-assessment exercises are readily available online or through career counseling services, and they can also be valuable tools for your young adult. These exercises prompt them to consider their skills, aptitudes, and preferred work environments.

- **You are the beacon they follow.** Be a positive role model for them by demonstrating resilience, curiosity, and a willingness to learn. Share stories of your own educational and career journey, including the challenges you faced and how you overcame them. Let them know that setbacks are always temporary and growth opportunities will happen. You can inspire your young adult to persevere in the face of obstacles and challenges.

- **Encourage them to step outside their comfort zone.** Remember when you were little and afraid to jump off the diving board? But then you finally took the plunge, which turned out to be amazing? That's kind of what your young adult's facing right now—a big, open pool of possibilities and maybe a little hesitation to jump in. Encourage your young adult to embrace exploration. Get them to try new things, discover hidden passions, and figure out what their strengths are. Support your young adult in exploring various interests, hobbies, and activities. Whether it's joining a club, trying out a new sport, or volunteering for a cause they care about,

65

encourage them to step out of their comfort zone and experience new things.

- **Give them high fives for their accomplishments.** When you acknowledge their hard work, it leaves them feeling great about themselves and gives them the confidence to try even more things. Celebrate your young adult's achievements, no matter how small. Acknowledge their efforts and successes, whether it's acing a test, landing a part-time job, or completing a project. That's all the motivation they need to stay focused, reinforcing the idea that their hard work is valued and appreciated. They get the idea that you see them, further strengthening your bond.

- **Do your research and find resources that can guide them.** Offer resources and guidance to help your young adult navigate their educational and career options. This could include researching colleges or vocational programs, exploring different career paths, or connecting them with mentors or professionals in fields they're interested in. Giving them access to information empowers them to make informed decisions about their future.

Navigating the Decision-Making Process With Your Young Adult Children

So, when it comes to making decisions with your young adult children, sometimes they might be unsure or nervous, and that's completely normal. You need to let them know you believe in their ability to figure things out. As they spread their wings and explore, here are some tips to help them with their decision-making:

1. Start by equipping your young adult with a range of resources to aid their educational exploration. These may include books, online databases, informational websites, and career guidance materials. Encourage them to explore various educational paths, such as traditional colleges and universities, vocational programs, technical institutes, or apprenticeships, for a comprehensive understanding of their options.

2. Next, offer them guidance on effective research techniques to gather relevant information about different educational institutions and programs. Teach them how to conduct thorough investigations into factors such as academic reputation, faculty expertise, program curriculum, campus facilities, extracurricular opportunities, and alumni success rates. They're becoming adults, so encourage them to utilize online resources, attend informational sessions, and reach out to current students or alumni for insights into their experiences.

3. Assist your young adult in navigating the intricate application processes associated with their chosen educational paths. This involves helping to clarify application requirements, deadlines, and procedures for each institution or program of interest but not taking control of the process. Help them compile necessary documents, such as transcripts, letters of recommendation, standardized test scores, and personal statements, ensuring they meet all submission guidelines. They'll need your encouragement to stay organized and proactive in completing their applications well in advance of deadlines.

4. Don't forget that they should be commandeering their own ship. While offering guidance and support, explain to your young adult the importance of taking ownership of their educational journey and making informed decisions that are in

line with their interests and goals. Encourage them to consider factors such as academic fit, career aspirations, geographic location, financial considerations, and personal preferences when evaluating their options. Encourage them to weigh the pros and cons of each choice and ultimately make the decision that feels right for them so they develop a sense of independence and self-reliance.

5. Remind your young adult that the path to education and career success may not always be straight and easy. Help them to understand how important it is to remain flexible and adaptable in the face of unexpected challenges or changes in direction. Life is unpredictable. So, teach them to keep an open mind and be willing to explore alternative pathways or adjust their plans as needed.

Letting Your Child Lead: Trusting Their Choices

Watching your children grow to this point in their lives has been an exciting experience for you as a parent. Sometimes, this transition feels almost unexpected. It can feel like their independent selves materialized overnight while you weren't watching, questioning all the past decisions you had to make on their behalf. This stage of their lives may come with some communication problems for both of you. But remember that your role as the parent is still intact.

Here are some tips to help you adapt your approach and become the supportive guide they need while they try to navigate life:

1. Learn to recognize and celebrate the uniqueness of your young adult's chosen path. Every human born into this world came in with their own set of talents, interests, and aspirations that may

lead them in unconventional directions. There is no "right" path to success. The sooner you accept it, the sooner you can embrace the diversity of experiences and perspectives that come from pursuing alternative routes.

2. Learn to respect your young adult's autonomy. How? Stop yourself from imposing your own aspirations or societal norms on their choices. Their journey is theirs alone, and they have the right to pursue their passions and interests without feeling pressured to conform to external expectations. Your job is to encourage them to follow their intuition and make decisions that align with their authentic selves, even if it means deviating from what society calls "normal."

3. Encourage their sense of independence and self-reliance by trusting their judgment and decision-making abilities. When they come to you, offer guidance and advice and leave it at that. Don't try to intervene or exert undue influence on their choices. Allow them the freedom to explore and experiment with different opportunities. After all, mistakes and detours are natural parts of the learning process.

4. Keep lines of communication open with your young adult, validating their feelings and offering empathy and understanding. Create a culture of trust and respect, and you can cultivate a strong parent-child relationship built on mutual respect and acceptance. So that even if they diverge from traditional paths, you can demonstrate your unwavering support for their autonomy and individuality.

Dealing With Failure and Setbacks

As the one with more life experience, please don't hesitate to explain to your young adult children that setbacks and failures don't make them incompetent but rather are components of the learning journey. Here are ways you can help them deal with failure and setbacks when they strike:

- **Teach them to embrace a growth mindset.** Encourage your young adult to view challenges as opportunities for personal and professional development. Tell them stories of your personal experiences that can teach them about learning from mistakes, adapting strategies, and refining approaches.

- **Remind them of how strong they are.** As your young adult navigates this exciting but sometimes overwhelming stage of life, remember to remind them just how strong they are so that when uncertainties hit, they'll remember they are strong enough to bounce back. Teach them to talk positively to themselves, like they would to a best friend. Talk to them about the benefits of taking deep breaths and meditation to help them stay calm during tough times.

- **Offer your young adult unwavering support.** As the storm rages in them, be a source of encouragement and reassurance, reminding them of their capabilities and past successes. Listen to their concerns and frustrations, and offer a supportive shoulder to lean on. This will help boost their resilience and empower them to persevere through life's inevitable obstacles.

- **Tell them about patience.** Patience is a virtue every young person needs to learn. Don't assume that your young adult understands this. Tell them that progress takes time, and that success cannot be achieved overnight. Help them to set realistic expectations, break goals down into manageable steps, and stay committed to their long-term aspirations.

The Art of Letting Go (While Still Being There)

It is possible to let go and still be there for someone, especially as a parent. At this point, your focus should be on maintaining ongoing communication, encouraging, and offering guidance to your young adult children while they make decisions about their lives. So, how exactly do you let go and still be there for your children?

- **Stay actively engaged.** Your child's life is not a football game; there isn't a break between halves. You need to remain actively involved in your young adult's journey, showing them your unwavering support and commitment to their growth and development. Regularly check in with them to inquire about their progress, challenges, and aspirations and show genuine interest in their endeavors.

- **Offer continuous support.** Your role as a parent also covers offering emotional, intellectual, and practical support to your young adult. Always be readily available to offer guidance, encouragement, and assistance whenever your adult child encounters any obstacles or uncertainties. They need you to be a reliable source of support for them.

- **Be more of a listening ear.** Effective communication is a two-way street that involves expressing your thoughts and concerns and actively listening to your young adult's perspectives and experiences. Be attentive and empathetic as they share their hopes, dreams, and fears with you. Even when you have plenty of things to say (as parents always do), don't interrupt or offer unsolicited advice. Just listen.

- **Use constructive feedback.** While offering support and encouragement, provide constructive feedback to help your young adult grow and develop. You can share insights gleaned from your own experiences or observations. Try to be tactful and diplomatic in your approach, focusing on constructive criticism rather than criticism.

- **Celebrate with them when things fall into place.** Take the time to acknowledge and celebrate your young adult's achievements, no matter how big or small. You should be genuinely proud of them; show it. You are highlighting their hard work, dedication, and perseverance. When you celebrate their achievements with them, you reinforce positive behaviors and boost their self-confidence and self-worth.

Believe it or not, your young adult children are under a lot of pressure from the world outside of the home, and when it comes to making decisions about their educational and career paths, they need all the guidance they can get. Ensure your children get the advice they need from you, especially now that you have the knowledge gained from this chapter. And when you can no longer be of help, introduce them to a professional. All your young adults need is to know that you love and support them no matter what. Keep being the best parent ever.

CHAPTER 5:

Navigating Conflict and Difficult Conversations

—❖—

Are you often finding yourself trapped in a cycle of repetitive arguments with your adult child? Do you catch yourself repeating the same phrases over and over again? Are you both drawn into negative patterns that seem all too familiar? Do your arguments always circle back to the same unresolved issues? Are hurtful words exchanged, leaving you both feeling regretful and misunderstood after every conversation? Do you feel your interactions go nowhere, leaving you frustrated and drained?

If you can relate to these frustrations, you're not alone. Many parents of emerging adults share similar struggles. But is there a way out of this cycle? Through research and counseling experience, there are several steps parents can take to minimize conflict with their emerging adult children and resolve disagreements when they arise.

William James once wisely said, "Whenever you're in conflict with someone, there is one factor that can make the difference between damaging your relationship and deepening it. That factor is attitude."

Conflict between parents and young adults is bound to happen. You're two different individuals with your own agendas, which often clash.

However, conflict isn't always a negative thing. It can help clarify issues in your relationship. But, if not handled carefully, it can leave both parties feeling drained and pessimistic about the future. No one wants a relationship defined by conflict and misunderstanding, yet it often happens when people get stuck in familiar patterns.

There is hope. Conflict can be managed and even transformed into a positive force in your relationship. As you dive into this topic, remain optimistic. The intensity and frequency of conflict will naturally decrease over time. Right now, your child is under a lot of stress. The demands of finding their place in society, relationships, and the workforce can lead to frequent conflicts. As the parent guiding them through these decisions, you may bear the brunt of their anger and frustration.

However, conflicts will lessen as your emerging adult becomes more comfortable with themselves and their future. Disagreements won't disappear entirely, but they'll become less intense and frequent. With this in mind, let's explore how to handle conflict in the present. Is there a way to make it less hurtful and more productive?

You and your young adult can navigate conflict in a way that leaves both of you feeling heard and respected. You don't have to resort to destructive patterns of hurling insults. Conflict can strengthen your relationship when managed effectively, increasing trust and understanding.

How you handle conflict can influence your emerging adult's journey toward self-acceptance and autonomy. Once they reach this point, they'll likely engage in fewer battles with you. So, it's crucial to manage conflict in a way that minimizes its impact and duration.

Getting the Right Mindset

Before you dive into specific strategies for improving your relationship with your young adult, take a moment to reflect deeply on past conflicts you've had with your child. Imagine those tense moments vividly, as if you're replaying a scene in a movie.

Recall a disagreement with your young adult that didn't go well. How did it start? Perhaps it began innocently enough, with a simple comment that inadvertently struck a nerve. Emotions ran high, and the situation escalated, leading to hurtful words and blame-throwing. Did you deliberately push each other's buttons, exploiting known vulnerabilities? Was it a familiar pattern, a well-worn dance you've performed before? And after all, did you feel a heavy weight of frustration, defeat, or perhaps even a profound misunderstanding? Reflect deeply on how you could have steered the interaction onto a more constructive path.

Now, contrast that with a conflict that ended positively. How did it begin? Perhaps it commenced with a calm and respectful discussion, with both parties genuinely listening to each other's perspectives. You each consciously avoided hurtful words, and communication flowed with mutual respect. You both actively contributed to finding a solution, seeking common ground despite your differences. Perhaps you even experienced a profound shift in understanding or respect for each other. In this scenario, your adult child might have taken the initiative to propose a solution themselves.

What made these two scenarios so different? The attitudes and behaviors exhibited during the successful encounter were likely markedly distinct from those in the unsuccessful one. In the positive exchange, you probably kept a sense of flexibility and openness while feeling genuinely respected and heard by each other. Collaboratively, you navigated through the disagreement, finding commonality amidst diversity. Both parties tried to empathize and see the situation from the other's perspective. Judgment and defensiveness were set aside, allowing space for genuine understanding and growth. Instead of resorting to monologues, you engaged in genuine dialogue, enriching your relationship.

The key takeaway here is that conflicts can either serve to divide or unite, depending on how they are approached.

Identify Triggers

In order to understand how conflicts can either turn sour or end well, try to focus on the steps that often lead to these results. When you think about the fights you have with your son or daughter, you might notice they follow a sort of dance routine. Some of these steps might feel familiar from arguments with other people, but some are probably unique to your relationship with your young adult. Once you see these patterns and understand how each step sets off reactions and counter-reactions, you can start to change things.

Being aware of what's going on is the key to making a change. If you want to improve how you handle conflicts, start by paying attention to yourself. The next time you find yourself in a familiar fight with your emerging adult, just watch yourself. You don't have to do anything differently yet; just step back and see the "dance" objectively. Look out for the things that tend to start conflicts between you. Notice how the argument unfolds and where things begin to fall apart. This awareness is the first step toward making things better. Remember, the goal isn't to avoid conflicts altogether but to find better ways to handle them so both you and your emerging adult feel heard and respected.

One significant trigger for fights between parents and emerging adults is money. Arguments can flare up when discussing spending, saving, or who should pay for what. Maybe you're worried because your daughter's choice of partners seems risky, but you know you can't control who she dates. You just want what's best for her. However, these disagreements often arise when discussing her love life.

Another trigger might be how your emerging adult chooses to live. For example, you might be frustrated because your son doesn't seem interested in finding a job and spends a lot of time hanging out with friends. You're worried about his future and finances, and these worries can lead to arguments between you.

Then, there are differences in values and goals. You might think it's essential for your child to focus on school and work, while they might value happiness and balance more. These differences can cause tension when discussing what they should do with their life. Recognizing these triggers allows you to discuss the issues before they become big arguments. For example, you can chat about money openly, understanding that your child might have different priorities and financial limitations. You can also express your concerns about their lifestyle in a supportive way, aiming to find common ground and understanding.

Overall, being aware of these triggers and handling them with care can help you and your emerging adult better deal with conflicts, leading to a stronger and happier relationship.

Have Realistic Expectations

Let's face it: Some things about your relationship with your emerging adult may never change, or at least not very quickly. Take temperamental differences, for example. Your messy son or daughter might just be untidy for life, never quite meeting your standards of cleanliness. Similarly, a perpetually pessimistic child might not transform into an eternal optimist, no matter how much you preach positivity. Accepting these differences and all their ups and downs is crucial for finding a conflict management approach that works.

When understanding your "conflict dance," you might already know the steps. But adding new steps, like agreeing to disagree or calming down, can be challenging. Choosing the "conscious path" over the temporary relief of shouting or hurling insults is tough. While those reactions might feel good in the moment, they ultimately do more harm than good. Choosing the conscious path, though harder, can lead to greater rewards in the long run.

Managing conflict doesn't mean giving in to the other side every time. You're entitled to your perspective, just as your emerging adult is entitled to theirs. But it does mean sacrificing the short-term satisfaction of venting your emotions for the long-term benefits of deeper understanding and a more respectful relationship.

Acknowledge honest differences without getting defensive. This allows both you and your emerging adult to move forward and appreciate the best in each other. It all starts with accepting that your emerging adult is different from you. The more they can establish their own identity and understand who they are, the less likely they'll be to engage in frequent battles with you. How you handle these conflicts can either support or hinder your emerging adult's journey toward self-discovery.

For example, suppose your adult child has a different approach to managing finances than yours. Maybe they prefer to spend money freely while you're more cautious. Instead of immediately jumping to criticism or trying to control their behavior, you could have an open conversation about your financial values and find a middle ground that respects both perspectives. This approach honors their autonomy while also fostering mutual understanding and respect.

Similarly, if you have differing views on career paths, you could explore reasons for their choices rather than dismissing their aspirations and offer support and guidance without imposing your own agenda. This approach encourages independence and self-expression while maintaining a supportive and nurturing environment within the family.

Overall, embracing these differences and approaching conflicts with patience, empathy, and open communication can strengthen your relationship and create a supportive foundation for growth and development.

Understand Your Conflict Management Style

Understanding how you and your son or daughter deal with conflict is essential for getting through disagreements without too much trouble. Everyone has their own way of handling arguments, and knowing this can really help things go more smoothly.

Think about how you usually react when things get heated. Are you the type to dive right into the argument, trying to convince your emerging adult you're right? Or maybe you're someone who steps back and gets upset. Understanding your type can give you a heads-up on how to handle conflicts better. Pay attention to whether you act differently at home compared to work or with family versus friends. And notice what sets you off—those are your "hot buttons."

Let's say your daughter keeps borrowing your car without asking. Instead of flipping out, take a second to realize you're feeling anxious because you're worried about her safety. Knowing this about yourself can help you talk to her more calmly.

Productive Dialogue, Active Listening, Negotiation

Participating in meaningful conversations, practicing active listening, and mastering negotiation skills are essential for building healthier relationships with your emerging adult. The following communication strategies will help you get through conflicts, encourage understanding, and create mutually beneficial outcomes:

Productive Dialogue

Productive dialogue involves constructive conversations to resolve conflicts and strengthen relationships. Instead of blaming or criticizing, focus on expressing your thoughts and feelings calmly and respectfully. Use "I" statements to communicate your perspective without placing blame. For example, instead of saying, "You never help with household chores," try saying, "I feel overwhelmed when I have to do all the household chores by myself."

Suppose your young adult consistently leaves dirty dishes in the sink despite your repeated reminders. Instead of starting the conversation with frustration or anger, initiate a dialogue by expressing how their actions impact you. For instance, you could say, "I understand you're busy, but when you leave dirty dishes in the sink, it adds to my workload and makes me feel overwhelmed. Can we find a solution together?"

Active Listening

Active listening involves fully concentrating on what the other person is saying without interrupting or formulating your response while they're speaking. Show genuine interest in understanding their perspective by maintaining eye contact, nodding, and providing verbal cues like "I see" or "That makes sense." Reflect on what you've heard to ensure clarity and demonstrate empathy.

Imagine your young adult expresses frustration about feeling pressured to follow your suggested career path. Instead of immediately defending your viewpoint, practice active listening by paraphrasing their concerns. You could say, "So, it sounds like you're feeling overwhelmed by the expectations I've set for your career. Is that right?" This approach shows that you value their perspective and opens the door for a more meaningful conversation.

Negotiation

Negotiation involves finding common ground and reaching mutually acceptable solutions through compromise and collaboration. Approach negotiations with an open mind and a willingness to explore different options. Focus on interests rather than positions, and be prepared to make concessions to achieve a win-win outcome.

Let's say your emerging adult wants to take a gap year before starting college, but you're concerned about the potential delay in their education. Instead of rejecting their request outright, start the negotiation by understanding the reasons for their decision. Perhaps they want to get work experience or travel before making a major life commitment. You could propose a compromise, such as agreeing to the gap year if they outline specific goals and plans for their time off.

Some Other Tips for Managing Conflict

Give Time and Space to Vent

When your adult child is upset, give them the opportunity to express their feelings fully. Sometimes, they just need to vent without immediately solving the issue. Let them speak without interruption, even if what they say triggers your own emotions. For instance, if your son is frustrated about his grades, allow him to share his feelings without jumping in with your opinions or solutions. Providing this space for them to express themselves shows that you value their emotions and are willing to listen.

For instance, suppose your daughter comes home upset because her best friend canceled plans at the last minute. Instead of immediately trying to fix the situation or offering advice, sit down with her and let her talk about how she feels. Say something like, "I'm here to listen if you want to talk about what happened." Doing this gives her the chance to unload her emotions and feel supported.

Respect Privacy

Conflicts can be sensitive, so it's best to keep them private whenever possible. Nobody likes having their personal issues aired in front of others. If you need to discuss something serious with your emerging adult, find a quiet spot away from prying ears. This shows respect for their privacy and avoids unnecessary embarrassment or tension.

Suppose your son is struggling with his mental health, and you want to talk to him about seeking help. Instead of bringing it up in front of the whole family, wait for a moment when you two can talk alone. Doing so ensures he feels comfortable and respected, making the conversation more productive.

Use "I" Language

When expressing your concerns or feelings, use "I" statements instead of "you" statements, shifting the focus away from blaming the other person and emphasizing your own experiences. For example, instead of saying, "You always leave your stuff everywhere," try saying, "I feel stressed when there's clutter around the house." As a less confrontational approach, it encourages open communication.

Your daughter frequently forgets to clean up after herself in the kitchen. Instead of criticizing her directly, express how it makes you feel. Say something like, "I feel overwhelmed when the kitchen is messy, and it's hard for me to cook dinner." Reacting this way instead helps her understand the impact of her actions without feeling attacked.

Avoid Big Generalizations and "Why" Questions

Using sweeping statements like "you never" or "you always" can make the other person feel defensive and unheard, and similarly, asking "why" questions can come across as accusatory and put the other person on the spot. Instead, focus on specific behaviors and use "how" questions to encourage dialogue and understanding.

Your son forgets to take out the trash one evening. Instead of saying, "You never remember to do your chores," try asking, "How come the trash didn't get taken out tonight?" This approach invites him to explain without feeling attacked.

Practice Active Listening

Active listening is a crucial skill in conflict resolution. Show that you're listening by nodding, keeping eye contact, and repeating what is said in your own words. This tactic demonstrates empathy and understanding, making them feel heard and valued.

Your daughter is upset about a fight with her friend. Instead of nodding, repeat what she said to show you understand. Say something like, "So you're feeling left out because your friend didn't invite you to her party, right?" Validating her feelings this way encourages further discussion.

Speak Calmly

Maintaining a calm demeanor during conflicts is critical to de-escalating tensions. Even if the other person gets loud or emotional, keep your voice and energy level steady. This will create a sense of security and reassurance, making it easier for both parties to communicate effectively.

Your son starts yelling about his curfew. Instead of raising your voice in response, stay calm and composed. Set a respectful tone for the conversation by saying something like, "I understand you're upset, but let's talk about this calmly."

Maintain Eye Contact

Eye contact is a powerful way to show that you're engaged and attentive during a conversation. However, don't stare aggressively, as this can be intimidating. Instead, hold respectful but non-aggressive eye contact to convey interest and understanding.

During a discussion about household responsibilities, keep eye contact with your emerging adult to show that you're actively listening and taking their concerns seriously. Doing this helps foster a sense of connection and mutual respect.

Repeat or Summarize

After your emerging adult shares their thoughts or feelings, repeat what they said in your own words. This shows you're actively engaged and ensures that you understand their perspective correctly. It also gives them the opportunity to clarify any misunderstandings and feel heard.

Your son expresses frustration about feeling overwhelmed with schoolwork. Repeat what he said to confirm your understanding. Show that you're attentive and empathetic to his concerns by saying something like, "So you're feeling stressed because of all the assignments piling up, is that right?"

Using these tips and understanding your conflict style can help you handle arguments better and build a stronger connection with your emerging adult. Remember, it's all about respect, patience, and listening to each other.

Rebuilding trust

Rebuilding trust and fixing relationships can be tricky, but it's crucial to keep your connection with your adult child strong. Whether there's been a big blow-up or just a series of minor misunderstandings, there are ways to mend the bond and move forward together.

1. **Acknowledge the pain:** Start by recognizing the hurt and upset feelings on both sides. You must show that you understand how your actions or words affect your child. For

example, if you missed your daughter's important event, acknowledge how much it must have hurt her.

2. **Take ownership:** Be brave enough to admit when you've messed up. Taking responsibility for your mistakes shows that you value the relationship and are willing to make amends. If you broke a promise to your son, apologize sincerely and without making excuses.

3. **Listen with care:** Create a space where your emerging adult feels safe to express their feelings. Listen to them without interrupting or judging. Let them know you're there to listen and understand their side of the story.

4. **Be dependable:** Follow through on your promises to show that you're reliable and trustworthy. Consistency in your actions over time helps rebuild trust. For instance, if you've promised to spend time with your son, make sure you stick to the plan.

5. **Respect boundaries:** Respect each other's personal boundaries. Talk openly about what's okay and what's not, and make sure to honor those boundaries. If your emerging adult needs space, give them the privacy they need.

6. **Consider counseling:** Sometimes, seeking guidance from a professional counselor who can provide neutral support and guidance can be helpful. Therapy sessions can offer a safe space to address underlying issues and work through challenges together.

7. **Team up:** Approach the process of rebuilding trust as a team effort. Involve your emerging adult in finding solutions and making decisions. Show them that you're committed to working together to strengthen your relationship.

8. **Patience is key:** Rebuilding trust takes time, so be patient with yourself and your emerging adult. Don't expect things to improve overnight, and be prepared for setbacks. Take things one step at a time and celebrate small victories together.

The End Goal

In the midst of conflict, it's crucial to ask yourself: What matters most? Is it about proving yourself right, or is it about finding common ground and moving forward together? This question becomes especially challenging when personal beliefs and values are involved. However, recognizing this fundamental question can help cut through the noise and focus on resolving the issue. For many parents, prioritizing their relationship with their emerging adult is paramount. It's about valuing connection over being right, and this mindset sets the stage for genuine communication and healing to take place.

Let's say you disagree with your daughter about her career choice. Instead of insisting on your perspective, consider whether preserving your relationship with her is more important than proving your point. This shift in mindset can pave the way for a more constructive conversation.

Being right isn't always as important as you think. How often does winning an argument lead to happiness or strengthen relationships? Parents sometimes get so fixated on winning small battles—like household chores or curfews—that they lose sight of the bigger picture. Ultimately, the goal of parenting is to raise independent, capable adults. Constantly asserting authority and insisting on being right may hinder this process rather than nurture it.

If your son disagrees with your curfew rules, instead of rigidly enforcing your stance, consider listening to his perspective and finding a compromise that respects both his autonomy and your concerns. This approach fosters mutual respect and understanding.

In conflicts with your emerging adult, the aim isn't to emerge as the victor but rather to find a balance that benefits both parties. This balance isn't about begrudging compromises but achieving a win–win outcome where both individuals feel heard and satisfied. While it may seem challenging, it's entirely possible with the right approach. Prioritizing understanding and respect over the need to be right creates an environment conducive to growth and mutual satisfaction.

For instance, if you and your emerging adult disagree about household responsibilities, consider brainstorming together to find a solution that meets your needs instead of insisting on your way. This collaborative approach fosters a sense of partnership and mutual respect.

Conflict, when managed effectively, can be a catalyst for growth and positive change. It highlights areas that need attention and provides opportunities for learning and development. Moreover, it encourages individuals to step out of their comfort zones and consider different perspectives, ultimately enriching life experiences. Suppose you and your adult child have differing opinions on social issues. Instead of avoiding the topic, engage in respectful discussions that challenge each other's viewpoints. Doing this opens up opportunities for personal growth and deeper understanding.

The goal isn't to eliminate conflict altogether but rather to navigate it in a way that encourages mutual respect and growth. Embracing differences and working together to find solutions that benefit both parties are key to building a mature, fulfilling relationship with your emerging adult.

CHAPTER 6:

Dealing with Setbacks in Your Adult Child's Life

—❖—

Some life challenges and situations come with setbacks. Guiding your adult child through them effectively and viewing them as part of self-discovery and independence is another responsibility you have as a parent. This chapter explores how your support can assist them during these challenging times. Your role here is to understand the fine line between being a pillar of strength and encouraging independence, which is vital for your young adult's personal development.

Parental Instincts

It's natural for parents to worry about their children. The love and concern you have for your child's well-being drives this parental instinct to immediately step in and try to fix things. These parental instincts are powered by your protective instincts, empathy, and the wisdom you've learned through your life experiences.

Protective Instinct

Your innate drive is hardwired into your biology and triggered when you perceive a threat to your adult child's well-being. This instinct surfaces to shield them from harm or distress when you feel your child facing big or small difficulties. Your instinctual response becomes to intervene and provide a solution to alleviate any potential harm or discomfort.

Empathy and Emotional Connection

The strong emotional bond you share with your child will always heighten your sense of empathy. You feel their pain, frustration, or disappointment on a deep level, compelling you to take immediate action to relieve their distress. The desire to spare your child from negative emotions is a powerful motivator behind the instinct to fix things.

Experience and Wisdom

Drawing from your life experiences, you have a wealth of knowledge and wisdom. Your instinct is to spare them from making the same mistakes you might have made.

Although these positive intentions can help your child in challenging times, it's also crucial to recognize potential downsides to this instinct when you overstep it.

Stifling Independence

When you start focusing on immediately fixing things and trying to take matters into your own hands, it can be seen by your adult child as you not trusting their abilities to tackle challenges independently.

Stepping in every time without giving your adult child enough time to make their next move will block their development of essential life skills and independence.

Furthermore, overprotecting your child by consistently intervening deprives them of opportunities to develop resilience. Facing setbacks and overcoming challenges is essential for their personal growth, and your constant interference may impede this natural process.

Unrealistic Expectations

Although your actions are well-intentioned, the efforts to fix everything might inadvertently communicate that mistakes are unacceptable. Unfortunately, this could create an atmosphere where your child feels pressured to meet unrealistic expectations, fearing failure.

Balancing this parental instinct to help your adult child is essential. Each situation needs to be taken on its own merits, and thinking before you act is what your adult child needs from you.

Offering Parental Guidance

When your child faces challenges or setbacks, taking the time to understand and validate their emotions helps create a supportive environment. Here's how you can effectively validate their experience and offer empathetic guidance:

Lend an Ear

As you already know, whether communicating or guiding your adult child during challenging times, listening with concern and being fully present is always crucial. Eye contact, positioning yourself in a way that conveys your undivided attention, and using cues like nodding and leaning slightly forward to show that you are actively engaged in the conversation.

Reflective Responses

After your adult child shares their thoughts and feelings, use reflective responses to show that you are genuinely trying to understand their perspective. Repeat key points to confirm your comprehension. Say your child expresses frustration. You can respond with something like, "It seems like you're feeling frustrated because of..."

Depending on the seriousness of the issue, you can also introduce empathetic statements that demonstrate your understanding of their emotional state. Phrases like "I can see how this situation is challenging for you" or "It must be tough to go through this" convey empathy and validation.

Avoiding Judgment

Create a judgment-free zone by refraining from immediate judgment or criticism. Everyone experiences challenges differently, and your role is to support rather than pass judgment.

Normalize Emotions

Reassure your child that experiencing a range of emotions is a natural part of being human. Normalize their feelings by stating it's okay to feel a certain way and there is no right or wrong in their emotions. Keep your emotions in check, as some scenarios can trigger emotions that won't be helpful.

Affirming Their Strengths

Take a moment to affirm your child's strengths. Remind them of their past successes in overcoming challenges, as it can help build their self-esteem and make them believe in their capabilities.

Ask Open-Ended Questions

Ask open-ended questions, inviting your adult child to share more about their experience. Questions like "Can you tell me more about what happened?" or "How did this make you feel?" can make them be more expressive and share their thoughts and emotions better. If the situation permits, you can also share relevant experiences from your own life. However, be cautious not to overshadow your child's feelings with your own story. Frame it as a way to connect and show that you, too, have faced challenges.

Remember, the goal is not just to hear your emerging adult but to actively listen and understand. Validating their experience and offering empathetic guidance is a gradual process that requires patience and a genuine commitment to building a trusting and supportive relationship.

Job-Searching Assistance

Navigating the job market can be daunting for young adults and anyone just beginning their professional journey. As parents, providing guidance and support during this crucial phase can significantly impact your young adult's success in finding employment. However, with rapidly changing job search strategies and increasing competition, assisting your young adult in their job search can be beneficial. Here are some practical tips and strategies to make job searching effective and efficient for your young adult:

- **Networking support:** Depending on their skills, interests, and preferences, offer guidance on how to be effective at networking. Help your adult child identify potential contacts within your professional circles or suggest joining relevant industry events for more exposure.

- **Job platforms:** Introduce them to reputable job-search platforms and assist in searching for job openings. If you are unfamiliar with online platforms, use the services of a relevant professional for guidance and tips on tailoring applications to specific positions. Although you can search for jobs through regular newspaper ads or similar media, using the internet to address these tasks has become the norm.

Resume-Writing Support

- **Review and edit:** Review your adult child's CV for improvement. You can suggest edits to their resume with constructive feedback on formatting, content, and language. However, ensure you are fully up-to-date on the latest formats businesses expect. Remind your emerging adult that different job positions might require them to tailor resumes to match specific job requirements.

Additional Practical Assistance Areas

- **Skill development programs:** Identify useful skill development programs or workshops that can add to your child's qualifications. These could include online courses, certifications, or workshops related to their field of interest.

- **Financial planning:** Share the information you gained from an earlier chapter on financial planning, especially if your young adult is in a transitional period. Remind them about budgeting, savings, and managing financial resources during job-seeking phases, as it's a struggle until they land a job.

- **Time management strategies:** Assist in developing effective time management strategies to balance job-searching activities, skill development, and personal well-being. Help them create a realistic schedule to stay organized.

Health and Wellness Support

- **Encourage healthy habits:** Keeping stress in check is necessary for good physical health during this challenging phase. Encourage them to exercise regularly and eat a balanced diet, as this is essential for positive mental health while job hunting.

- **Access to healthcare resources:** Ensure your young adult has healthcare resources. Get them familiar with health insurance options or connect them with relevant services. You can also share your experiences when necessary for better guidance.

Support Groups

- **Find peers:** Guide your emerging adult to finding relevant support groups or professional associations related to their field of interest. They can also join related online groups and forums to better understand the industry they are interested in joining.

Counseling

- **Professional counseling services:** If needed, consider recommending professional counseling services to provide specialized career guidance and emotional support. Connect them with reputable counselors or therapists who specialize in career-related challenges.

- **Family discussions:** Initiate open and supportive discussions within the family. Allow your adult child to express their concerns and aspirations and be receptive to their needs.

Don't forget that offering practical assistance means helping your young adult navigate challenges independently while knowing they have your support. Tweaking your assistance to their specific needs and keeping the lines of communication open creates a collaborative approach to their personal and professional development.

Balancing Support With Independence

Balancing support with independence is delicate and nuanced and requires a thoughtful approach. It involves creating an environment where your child feels encouraged to navigate challenges while knowing they have a reliable support system. Let's explore the intricacies of achieving this balance:

Open Communication

Create a safe space by helping to establish an open and non-judgmental environment where your child feels comfortable expressing their thoughts and concerns. Let them know that your intention is to support, not control.

Encourage honest dialogue and actively encourage open communication by asking open-ended questions. Doing this allows your child to share their experiences, aspirations, and challenges, fostering a sense of trust.

Clarify Expectations

Clearly communicate your expectations and, equally importantly, seek to understand your child's expectations. It will help establish a framework for collaboration and avoid misunderstandings.

Empower Decision-Making

Let your child initiate the decision-making processes, especially those decisions directly impacting their life. Whether it's career choices, educational pursuits, or personal goals, giving them a say recognizes their maturity.

Encourage Problem-Solving Skills

When faced with challenges, encourage your child to brainstorm solutions rather than jumping in and providing immediate answers. Guide them through the process of critical thinking and decision-making. Remind them of instances where they successfully resolved issues on their own, reinforcing their capability and boosting confidence in their problem-solving skills.

Respect Boundaries

Respect your child's need for personal space and independence. Avoid intrusive behavior and trust them to manage certain aspects of their life, even if it means making mistakes and learning from them.

Celebrate Achievements

Don't forget to celebrate your child's achievements, no matter how small. This positive reinforcement reinforces their sense of accomplishment and independence. Acknowledge their efforts rather than solely focusing on outcomes.

Encourage Self-Reflection

Encourage your child to self-reflect, which involves understanding their strengths, weaknesses, and goals. Promoting self-awareness lays a solid foundation for making informed decisions independently.

Adapt to Changing Needs

Recognize that the level of support your child needs may change over time. Be adaptable and responsive to their evolving needs, adjusting your role as a supporter accordingly.

Balancing support with independence requires a deep understanding of your child's personality, strengths, and challenges. Striking the right balance can be achieved by continuously fine-tuning your approach, ensuring that your support acts as a scaffold for their growth rather than a constraint on their independence. Being attuned to their needs, respecting boundaries, and maintaining open communication creates a foundation for a healthy relationship.

Setting Realistic Expectations

Setting realistic expectations is a crucial aspect of navigating setbacks. Here are the practical steps you can take to set realistic expectations for your adult child to better navigate their journey toward independence:

Understanding the Situation

Start by thoroughly understanding the current situation. Assess your child's strengths and weaknesses and the external factors influencing the setback. These could relate to their career, personal relationships, or other aspects of their life.

For example, if the setback is in their career, consider factors like market conditions, industry trends, and your child's specific skills and qualifications.

Identifying Limitations and Resources

After you understand the situation, try to recognize any limitations or constraints your child may face together. These could include financial constraints, time limitations, or gaps in their skills and knowledge. Say your child is pursuing a career change. Acknowledge the financial constraints they might face during this transitional period. In a situation like this, setting expectations that fit within their financial reality will benefit them and enable them to create a more realistic and achievable plan.

Aligning Expectations With Goals

Get together with your child to set goals. Always be careful not to prescribe them but to work on them together. Understand their long-term ambitions and break them down into smaller, manageable goals. Match expectations to these goals, and make sure that each step is feasible within a reasonable timeframe. For example, if your adult child wants to enter a competitive field, break down the goal into smaller milestones like getting relevant certifications, practical experience, and growing their professional network.

You can use the SMART goal strategy to divide long- and short-term goals into smaller, measurable milestones that have to be achieved within a certain timeframe.

Considering External Factors

Acknowledge external factors that may impact reaching the goals. These can include economic conditions in the region, market fluctuations, or unexpected life events. Furthermore, in a rapidly changing job market, recognize that securing a position may take longer than anticipated. Setting realistic expectations involves understanding the dynamic nature of the external job market and preparing for potential challenges.

Encouraging Flexibility

Encourage your adult child to develop a flexible mindset that allows for adjustments to the plan as needed. Recognize that setbacks might mean changes need to be made to their expectations, and encourage your child to view adaptability as a strength. Say your child faces unexpected challenges in a new job. Encourage them to be flexible. They might have to adjust their career progression timeline or seek additional training to address these specific challenges. Furthermore, regularly check in with your child to discuss their progress and any adjustments needed to their goals or expectations.

Encouraging Patience and Persistence

Stress the value of patience and persistence in the face of setbacks. Encourage your child to view setbacks as temporary obstacles and to look at challenges as opportunities for growth. For example, when your child faces initial rejections in job applications, emphasize that they are more common than not at the beginning of any career. Encourage them to keep trying and see setbacks as stepping stones to eventual success.

Encouraging Self-Care

Encouraging self-care is a vital aspect of supporting your adult child through setbacks. It involves promoting practices that contribute to their physical, mental, and emotional well-being during challenging times. Let's explore encouraging self-care in extreme detail, incorporating examples for clarity:

Defining Self-Care

Self-care is clearly defined as a holistic approach to well-being. It includes activities that nurture physical health, emotional balance, and mental resilience and that just make you feel good and relaxed. Emphasize that self-care is not indulgent but a necessary investment in their overall health. Help your adult child understand that self-care includes things like regular exercise, healthy eating, sufficient sleep, mindfulness, and activities that bring joy and relaxation.

Customizing Self-Care Practices

Encourage your child to customize self-care practices based on what they enjoy doing. What works for one person may not work for another, so promoting personalized approaches ensures sustainability. For example, if they enjoy nature, suggest activities like hiking, gardening, or simply spending time outdoors. For those who prefer indoor activities, meditation, reading, or an artistic hobby can be effective as a self-care strategy.

Prioritizing Physical Health

Stress the importance of regular exercise in maintaining physical health. Physical activity not only boosts mood through endorphin release but also improves overall well-being. Encourage your adult child to find an exercise routine they enjoy, whether it's jogging, yoga, swimming, or team sports. Suggest a joint activity, like going for a walk together or doing any of the activities shared above, as an ideal way to combine healthy activity and open communication opportunities.

Emphasizing Mental Well-Being

Highlight the benefits of mindfulness practices, like meditation or deep-breathing exercises, in promoting mental well-being. These practices can help manage stress and enhance emotional resilience. You can recommend mindfulness apps or guided meditation sessions that your child can integrate into their daily routine. You can also share your own experiences with mindfulness and tell them what worked for you.

Ensuring Adequate Rest

Emphasizing the importance of quality sleep and the role it plays in reliable cognitive function and emotional balance is a no-brainer. Discuss the impact sleep has on overall health and managing stress. Help your emerging adult set a regular sleep routine with consistent bedtime and a comfortable sleep environment, and avoid stimulating activities before bedtime.

Balancing Work and Personal Life

Just like you read about work–life balance earlier, discuss the necessity of setting boundaries between work and personal life. Overworking contributes significantly to burnout, while a healthy work–life balance promotes sustainable well-being. Encourage your child to establish clear work hours, breaks, and leisure time boundaries. This balance might involve creating a dedicated workspace, setting specific work hours, and unplugging from work-related communication during personal time.

Cultivating Healthy Relationships

Healthy relationships are also a factor that contributes to overall well-being. Encourage your child to nurture existing connections and build supportive relationships. You can suggest activities encouraging social interactions, like joining clubs, attending social events, or reconnecting with friends. Remind them that positive relationships aid in building emotional resilience.

Seeking Professional Support

Normalize seeking professional help when needed. Discuss the value of counseling or therapy as a resource for managing stress, navigating challenges, and enhancing emotional well-being. For example, if your child is experiencing persistent stress or emotional difficulties, encourage them to explore counseling services.

Limiting Negative Influences

Discuss the impact of media on mental well-being and how necessary it is to manage how much your adult child exposes themselves to negative news or social media. Suggest setting boundaries on the time spent consuming news or social media and encourage them to do things that bring joy instead. Demonstrating this behavior yourself can serve as a powerful example.

Promoting Joyful Activities

Encourage your child to prioritize activities that bring joy and fulfillment. Hobbies and leisure pursuits contribute to a sense of purpose and balance in life. If your child enjoys painting, reading, or playing a musical instrument, support their engagement in these activities. Actively participating with them in shared hobbies can enhance the experience.

Developing a Self-Care Plan

Help your child to draw up a personalized self-care plan. This plan should include specific activities for physical, mental, and emotional well-being. Encourage them to regularly reassess and adjust the plan based on their evolving needs.

Instilling a Positive Mindset

Have discussions about how to keep positive, even in difficult times. The easiest way to do this is to focus on gratitude and be thankful for how far they have come already. Suggest keeping a gratitude journal, where your adult child can jot down things for which they are thankful daily. Share your own experiences where cultivating a positive mindset helped you overcome challenges to help them.

CHAPTER 7:

Maintaining Strong Family Ties through Activities and Traditions

—❖—

Family traditions like holiday gatherings, milestone celebrations, and reunions are more than just events—they're opportunities for families to connect and create lasting memories. However, they can, at times, also be overwhelming. You know how it goes—endless conversations about the latest news or family disagreements that seem to pop up out of nowhere. And the mountain of dishes to wash afterward.

Thanksgiving, Christmas, and other big holidays are like a trip down memory lane for families gathered around the table, reliving old emotions and experiences. The smells wafting from the kitchen can instantly transport parents back to when their children were little, giving them a sense of control they haven't felt in years. But for grown children, it's a different story. They don't like feeling powerless or judged like they did when they were younger, and tensions can rise quickly.

Adult children who come home only for the holidays face even more pressure. Returning home means confronting old conflicts and dynamics they thought they left behind. It's tough not to revert to feeling like a child again, especially when parents treat them that way.

The nostalgia triggered by the smell of turkey and yams makes breaking free from old habits even harder.

As parents, it's important to recognize that your family is constantly evolving. Change is inevitable, whether it's welcoming new members through marriage or dealing with the challenges of divorce and loss. If you don't adapt your traditions to fit these changes, they can feel more like obligations than joyful celebrations.

But as your children grow older, their priorities and schedules may shift. They might want to bring a friend to Thanksgiving dinner or spend Christmas with their significant other's family. It's all part of them spreading their wings and becoming independent.

When your adult children marry or cohabit, their families expand, and you need to respect their decisions about these new dynamics. Instead of competing with your in-laws for holiday time, it makes life smoother to support your children's choices. And when it comes to hosting family gatherings, your adult children need to take on some of that responsibility themselves. After all, they need the practice, which helps them feel more invested in the family traditions.

Family traditions are meant to bring you closer together and create meaningful experiences. So, instead of clinging to how things have always been done, embrace change and find new ways to celebrate and connect with our loved ones. And if you ever feel nostalgic for the past, just take a look at those old family photos—they're a reminder of how much you've grown and how far you've come.

Prioritize Regular Quality Time

Establishing regular family time is crucial for maintaining strong connections and creating lasting memories. Whether you set aside one evening a week or a weekend afternoon, having designated family time can help strengthen your bond and keep your relationship thriving. Forget about movie nights and game nights with the children—now it's about finding activities that resonate with your grown children and cater to their interests and schedules. So, what can you do during your designated family time? Here are some ideas to get you started:

Attend Local Events

Check out community concerts, art fairs, or food festivals together. It's a great way to spend time outside the house and enjoy each other's company while exploring new experiences. For example, you could attend a music festival in the park or visit an art gallery opening in your neighborhood.

Get Active Together

Instead of playing board games, why not go for a hike, bike ride, or play a round of golf? Staying active as a family not only promotes physical health but also provides opportunities for meaningful conversations and shared experiences. Consider signing up for a family-friendly 5k race or joining a recreational sports league together.

Cook and Dine Together

Host a themed dinner night where everyone pitches in to prepare a meal. Whether it's trying out new recipes or revisiting family favorites, cooking and eating together can be a fun and rewarding way to bond. You could have a taco night where each family member creates their own custom taco, or try making homemade pizzas with various toppings.

Support Each Other's Interests

Attend your adult children's performances, art exhibits, or sports games. Showing up and cheering them on demonstrates your love and support, and it's a great way to connect with them over their passions. Whether it's a local theater production, an art show, or a basketball game at their alma mater, make an effort to be there for your adult children.

Start a Joint Project

Whether it's tackling a DIY home improvement project, starting a garden, or planning a family vacation, working together toward a common goal fosters teamwork and strengthens your family bond. Consider renovating a room in your house together, planting a vegetable garden in your backyard, or researching and planning a dream vacation as a family.

Share Household Responsibilities

Assign chores and tasks that everyone can contribute to, regardless of age. Whether it's cooking dinner, doing laundry, or tidying up the house, working together as a team promotes a sense of unity and responsibility. You could create a rotating chore chart where each family member is responsible for a different task each week or have a weekly family cleaning session where everyone pitches in to tidy up the house.

Have Regular Family Meetings

Set aside time to discuss important family matters, plan upcoming events, and check in with each other. It's a chance to voice concerns, share achievements, and ensure everyone feels heard and valued. Consider holding monthly family meetings where you gather around the dining table to discuss topics like family finances, upcoming vacations, and any issues or concerns that need to be addressed.

Prioritize Downtime

These days, it's essential to carve out time for relaxation and rejuvenation. You could schedule a tech-free day, plan a weekend getaway, or simply unwind at home together, prioritizing downtime as a family to recharge and reconnect. Or you might plan a family staycation where you spend a weekend relaxing at home, indulging in your favorite hobbies, and enjoying quality time together without any distractions.

Remember, the key is consistency. Make family time a non-negotiable part of your schedule, and prioritize it just as you would any other commitment. By investing in regular family time, you're investing in the health and happiness of your relationships for years to come.

Cultivate and Uphold Family Traditions

Whether it's a cherished holiday ritual, a crazy in-family annual tradition, or a simple routine that brings everyone together, family traditions play a crucial role in strengthening family bonds and creating lasting memories. They're the glue that holds families together through thick and thin.

But what exactly are family traditions, and why are they so important? Family traditions are the rituals, customs, and activities passed down from generation to generation. They can be as simple as Sunday dinners or as elaborate as annual family vacations. Regardless of their size or scope, these traditions serve as anchors, providing comfort, stability, and a sense of belonging.

Take, for example, the Pritchett-Dunphy family from the popular sitcom "Modern Family." From their annual Thanksgiving football game to their quirky Halloween costumes, the Pritchett-Dunphys have many traditions that unite them and define who they are as a family. And while their traditions may seem over-the-top at times, they're a testament to the power of rituals in creating shared experiences and strengthening relationships.

But you don't need a TV show to understand the importance of family traditions. In fact, many families have their own particular traditions that are just as meaningful. For some, it's a weekly movie night where everyone gathers on the couch with popcorn and blankets. For others, it's a yearly camping trip where they disconnect from the outside world and reconnect with each other around the campfire.

Some families have traditions rooted in their cultural or religious heritage. For example, a Jewish family might celebrate Hanukkah by lighting the menorah and exchanging gifts. A Mexican-American family might honor Dia de los Muertos with a traditional altar and a feast of tamales and pan de muerto. These traditions connect families to their roots and provide a sense of pride and belonging.

Of course, family traditions don't have to be elaborate or formal to be meaningful. Even something as simple as a movie night or a morning walk can become a cherished tradition if done consistently. The key is to find activities that resonate with your family and bring you closer together.

But cultivating and upholding family traditions isn't always easy. It can be challenging to carve out time for these rituals amid work, college, and other obligations, so priorities need to be set to make them a non-negotiable part of your family's routine.

One way to do this is to involve everyone in the planning process. Sit down as a family and brainstorm ideas for new traditions or ways to adapt existing ones to fit your current circumstances better. Maybe you can't go on your annual beach vacation this year, but you can still have a family barbecue in the backyard or a movie marathon at home.

It's also necessary to be flexible and open to change. As families grow and evolve, so too should their traditions. What worked for you when your kids were young may not be feasible now that they're adults with their own lives and responsibilities. Instead of clinging to the past, embrace the opportunity to create new traditions that reflect your family's current dynamics and interests.

Of course, the process is not always a smooth one. Differences in opinion, conflicting schedules, and changing priorities can all threaten to derail even the most beloved rituals. But with patience, communication, and a healthy dose of humor, families can overcome these challenges and continue to uphold their traditions for generations to come.

In the end, it's the shared experiences and cherished memories that make family traditions so special. Whether it's baking cookies together at Christmas or going on a family road trip every summer, these rituals create a sense of continuity and connection that can withstand the test of time. So here's to the traditions that make you who you are and the families that keep them alive.

Include Adult Children in Decision-Making

Involving adult children in decision-making processes can be a game-changer for family dynamics. It's not just about making them feel valued and respected—it's about encouraging a sense of ownership, empowerment, and connection that can strengthen family bonds and keep everyone engaged in each other's lives.

When adult children are included in decision-making, they'll feel like active participants in the family rather than just passive observers. They're more likely to feel invested in the outcomes of those decisions and more inclined to contribute their ideas and perspectives. Plus, involving them in decision-making can help bridge the generation gap and foster open communication and mutual understanding.

Take, for example, the Johnson family. Instead of making all the decisions about their annual family vacation themselves, they hold a family meeting where everyone gets to weigh in on potential destinations, activities, and budgets. Doing this ensures everyone's preferences are considered and gives adult children a sense of ownership and responsibility for the trip.

Similarly, the Patel family has a tradition of including their adult children in major financial decisions, like buying a new car or renovating their home. Involving them in the process from start to finish imparts valuable financial literacy skills and reinforces the idea that everyone's input is valuable and necessary.

But involving adult children in decision-making isn't just about practical matters—it's also about creating opportunities for meaningful interactions and sharing experiences. For example, the Garcia family has a tradition of holding monthly "family brainstorming sessions" where they come together to discuss potential ideas for outings, holiday traditions, and other activities.

Involving adult children in decision-making can also lead to some memorable and exciting experiences. Take, for instance, the Smith family, who decided to let their adult children plan their parents' 40th wedding anniversary celebration. From choosing the venue, designing the invitations, and organizing the entertainment and menu, the adult children took charge. They created a truly unforgettable event that brought the whole family together.

Ultimately, involving adult children in decision-making is more than just making them feel like grown-ups—it's about building a stronger, more cohesive family unit. Giving them a seat at the table and empowering them to contribute their ideas and opinions fosters a sense of responsibility and independence and creates opportunities for meaningful connections and shared memories.

So the next time you're faced with a decision that affects the whole family, why not invite your adult children to join the conversation? You might be surprised by the ideas they bring to the table and the bonds that are strengthened in the process. After all, when everyone has a say, everyone feels invested—and that's what family is all about.

Nurture Sibling Relationships

Nurturing sibling relationships is just as important for adult children as it is for younger ones. While siblings may grow apart as they enter adulthood and pursue their own paths, investing in their relationship can lead to a lifelong source of support, companionship, and understanding.

Have Frequent Sibling Hangouts

Encourage your adult children to spend quality time together by hosting regular sibling gatherings. Whether it's a monthly dinner at a favorite restaurant, a weekend getaway, or an annual family reunion, these gatherings provide opportunities for siblings to reconnect and strengthen their bond. Consider taking inspiration from the Braverman siblings in the TV show "Parenthood," who make it a priority to come together for family dinners and celebrations despite their busy lives.

Heart-to-Heart Talks

Encourage open and honest communication between siblings by creating opportunities for meaningful conversations. Organize structured discussions on topics like family history, shared memories, or future goals. You could even set aside time during family gatherings for siblings to share updates on their lives, discuss challenges they're facing, and offer support and advice to one another.

Team Up on Projects

Encourage collaboration and teamwork between siblings by inviting everyone to take part in shared projects or activities, providing that your adult children are comfortable sharing. Whether planning a surprise party for a parent's milestone birthday, tackling a home renovation project together, or starting a family business, working toward a common goal can strengthen the sibling bond and create lasting memories. Encourage your adult children to brainstorm ideas and take ownership of the project from start to finish.

Celebrate Each Other's Wins

Recognize and celebrate each sibling's milestones and achievements to show their successes are valued and appreciated. Whether it's graduating from college, landing a new job, or starting a family, make an effort to acknowledge these important moments in each sibling's life. Consider organizing a joint celebration or sending a heartfelt card or gift to mark the occasion.

Keep Traditions Alive (or Start New Ones)

Establishing new family traditions can help adult siblings stay connected and create shared memories. Whether it's a monthly game night, an annual holiday cookie-baking extravaganza, or a summer camping trip, these traditions provide opportunities for siblings to come together. Get creative and involve your adult children in brainstorming ideas for new traditions that reflect their interests and preferences.

By implementing these ideas, parents can play a vital role in nurturing sibling relationships among their adult children. Whether through regular gatherings, heart-to-heart talks, collaborative projects, or shared traditions, investing in these relationships can create a strong foundation for lifelong connection and support. After all, siblings are often your first and longest-lasting friends—so why not make the effort to keep those bonds strong?

Support Their Major Milestones

As parents, one of the greatest joys in life is witnessing your children achieve major milestones. From graduations to job promotions to buying their first home, these moments mark significant achievements in their journey to adulthood. Here are some ways you can show your support and celebrate these milestones with your adult children:

Throw a Graduation Bash (Even if It's Virtual)

When your adult child graduates from college or completes a degree program, it's time to break out the party hats and celebrate their hard work and dedication. Throw a graduation bash to honor their achievement, whether it's a backyard barbecue, a fancy dinner at their favorite restaurant, or a virtual celebration with family and friends.

Offer Career Guidance and Encouragement

Navigating the professional world can be daunting for young adults, so offer your support and guidance as they embark on their career journey. Ask them if they would like help polishing their resume, practicing for job interviews, and exploring different career paths. Share your experiences and insights, and encourage them to forge their own path and pursue their passions. If your child lands their dream job, celebrate their success with a congratulatory dinner or a toast at home. You could even treat them to a "survival kit" filled with office essentials and a humorous note to lighten the mood.

Help With Home Sweet Home

Buying their first home is a major milestone for many young adults, and it's an exciting time to offer your support and assistance. Help them navigate the home-buying process by offering advice on finding the right neighborhood, securing financing, and negotiating with sellers. Offer to lend a hand with moving day or help them spruce up their new space with some DIY home improvement projects. To add a humorous touch, consider giving them a "homeowner's survival kit" filled with practical items like a toolbox, duct tape, and a humorous guidebook on DIY disasters.

Celebrate Relationship Milestones

Whether your adult child is getting engaged, married, or welcoming a new addition to the family, these relationship milestones are cause for celebration. Offer your support and encouragement as they embark on this new chapter of their lives. Attend their engagement party, wedding, or baby shower, and offer to help with the planning and preparations. If your child is getting married, consider sharing some lighthearted marriage advice or funny anecdotes from your own relationship. And don't forget to raise a glass and toast their love and happiness!

Be Their Biggest Cheerleader

Above all, be your adult child's biggest cheerleader and source of support as they navigate life's ups and downs. Whether they're starting a new job, pursuing further education, or facing challenges, let them know that you're always there for them. Offer words of encouragement, lend a listening ear, and celebrate their victories—big and small.

Remember, life is full of big and small milestones, and your role as a parent is to support and celebrate your adult children every step of the way.

Use of Technology When Physically Distant to Maintain Connections

In today's digital age, staying connected with your loved ones has never been easier, thanks to the wide array of technological tools and platforms available. If your adult children live miles away or lead busy lives, leveraging technology is essential for maintaining strong and meaningful connections. From social media platforms to video chat apps to virtual activities, there are countless ways for you to stay in touch with your adult children, even when physical distance separates you. However, don't fall into the trap of becoming intrusive, which is so easily possible with social media use.

Snapchat for Quick Updates

Snapchat may be known for its disappearing messages, but it's also a powerful tool for staying connected. You can create a Snapchat account and encourage your kids to send you snaps throughout the day, providing quick updates on their activities, adventures, and everyday moments. Whether it's a funny selfie, a scenic view, or a glimpse into their daily routine, these snaps offer a lighthearted way to stay in the loop, even from a distance.

Instagram Stories for Daily Updates

Instagram Stories provide another avenue for staying connected with adult children daily. You can follow your children on Instagram and watch their Stories to see highlights from their day, behind-the-scenes moments, and glimpses into their interests and hobbies. You can try to engage with their content and send supportive messages or emojis to show your interest and support, fostering a sense of closeness and connection.

TikTok for Shared Laughs

If your children are into TikTok, why not join the fun? You can create your own TikTok account and follow your kids to watch their videos and engage with their content. From dance challenges to lip-syncing duets to funny skits, TikTok offers endless opportunities for shared laughs and bonding experiences. You can even try your hand at creating your own TikTok videos together, creating memories and strengthening your relationship in the process.

Discord for Virtual Movie Nights

Discord isn't just for gamers—it's also a fantastic platform for hosting virtual movie nights with your children. You can create a private Discord server and invite your kids to join, using the screen-sharing feature to stream a movie or TV show together. With real-time chat for reactions and commentary, it's like having a movie night in the comfort of your own home, no matter how far apart you may be.

Netflix Teleparty for Shared Viewing

Netflix Teleparty (formerly Netflix Party) offers another option for watching movies and shows together online. You can install the Teleparty browser extension, choose a movie or show to watch, and invite your children to join the party. Syncing your viewing experience and chatting in real-time means you can enjoy shared entertainment and meaningful conversations, even when you're physically apart.

Family WhatsApp Group for Daily Chats

Creating a family WhatsApp group chat is an excellent way for parents to stay in touch with their adult children. You can share updates, photos, and news from their day-to-day lives and encourage your kids to do the same. With the convenience of instant messaging and the intimacy of a private group chat, WhatsApp offers a seamless way to keep a sense of closeness and connection, no matter where everyone is in the world.

Virtual Book Club for Shared Interests

For parents and adult children who share a love of reading, starting a virtual book club together is a fantastic way to stay connected and engaged. You can choose a book to read each month, set up a group chat or video call to discuss your thoughts and impressions and enjoy lively conversations about plot twists, character development, and favorite quotes.

Online Cooking Classes for Virtual Hangouts

Cooking classes aren't just for in-person experiences—they can also be enjoyed together online. You can sign up for virtual cooking classes or workshops and schedule regular sessions with your children. Whether you're learning how to make homemade pasta, perfecting your sushi-rolling skills, or mastering the art of pastry baking, cooking together over video chat offers an interactive way to bond and create delicious memories. Plus, parents and kids can enjoy the fruits of their labor together, even if they're miles apart.

Family is where the heart is. Whether you share laughs over Sunday dinner or send goofy snaps on Snapchat, every moment counts. Just remember to keep the love flowing and the connections strong—after all, life's too short for dull family gatherings and awkward silences. So spice things up, embrace the chaos, and make memories that'll last a lifetime.

CONCLUSION

—❖—

As the saying goes, relationships need to be nourished to flourish. Young adult children may need help understanding this fact since their sole focus would be to build their identity and find a purpose. As a parent, you have to take the pains to maintain strong family ties. After noticing your perseverance and love, your children may one day follow suit and contribute their share to the relationship.

Humans are constantly evolving, and your children are no different. Their evolution takes a giant leap post-adolescence. You need to keep pace with them to maintain the bond. The first step is to accept that your parent–child dynamics are evolving. Your young adults may not react to the same kind of parenting as you have been doing for so long.

The second thing is not to do anything that might prevent that evolving dynamic from developing, especially if it's in an attempt to change them. They may not react positively to your attempts. Change yourself instead of trying to change them. Adapt to their transformation rather than resisting it. Be like a chameleon that doesn't try to change the rock it's perched on but adopts its color to protect itself.

Communication forms the crux of this changing dynamic. You need to let your children know you are with them through thick and thin. Don't just let them guess at it from your actions. Tell them directly they have you to fall back on if they encounter any hurdles. Be as open and honest as possible without any expectation on your side.

Acknowledge that your adult children have become independent. They have their own sets of opinions, morals, and choices. You may not always agree with them, but you need to accept them. Respecting their autonomy is crucial to avoid needless conflicts.

Avoid being overly controlling or intrusive. Think of them as your equals, as friends, but don't be overly friendly either. Be their guide and a calming presence they can turn to in times of both joy and sorrow.

Active listening is an integral part of communicating with your children. Give your full attention when they are speaking. Engage all your senses and reciprocate with gestures or body language from time to time. Validate their feelings and perspectives, even if you don't necessarily agree with them. Avoid interrupting them or dismissing their opinions.

Offer your support and encouragement without being overbearing. Let your adult children know you are there for them if they need guidance or assistance. At the same time, you should give them space to handle their challenges and decisions. In short, you should help them only if they ask for it.

If you are communicating with them openly but they aren't sharing their thoughts with you, they may not feel comfortable expressing themselves. Avoid being judgmental while you're speaking. Honesty is one thing, but you also need to be mindful of their feelings and sensitivities.

Setting boundaries is an essential aspect of a healthy relationship. Admittedly, love has no boundaries, but relationships need boundaries to survive, no matter how strong. Establish clear boundaries in your communication with them to avoid any future conflicts. Respect their limits as well, and be mindful of not overstepping or intruding into their personal space. Love them unconditionally, but respect their privacy.

Indeed, at this age, they may keep many things from you. If you are too intrusive, they may never share anything with you. The key is to trust them implicitly. Trust that you have done your job in the past well enough that they will make the right decisions, cope with challenges that cross their path, and learn from their mistakes. Only then, if it becomes too much for them to handle, will they approach you for help.

Appreciate their accomplishments, no matter how big or small. Celebrate successes and milestones and tell them you are proud of them.

Despite your efforts, conflict may occur. They are inevitable in any relationship, but it's essential to handle disagreements constructively—approach conflicts with a willingness to understand each other's perspectives and work together to find solutions.

Stay connected with your adult children through regular contact, whether it's through phone calls, video chats, or in-person visits. Keeping in touch helps strengthen your bond and ensures that you remain involved in each other's lives. It doesn't matter how many conflicts you are embroiled in. At the end of the day, with effective communication, your bond will be stronger than ever.

Granted, your children are becoming independent, but you need to ensure they have all the tools to remain independent. When they realize what the world requires of them, they will turn to you for guidance. Give it freely without any judgments or holding anything against them.

Teach them the basics of handling their finances. Earning and saving money is a critical life skill. Go on to explain advanced money management strategies, like budgeting, investing, planning taxes, and so on.

Financial organizing naturally leads to problem-solving. What if they end up spending more than they earn? In turn, what if they make more money than they can spend? Show them what to do in each extreme case.

Healthcare is a key skill that will help your adult child to achieve all their goals. At their age, they usually won't make it their first priority. The negative impacts of health negligence aren't immediate. You should help them realize what may happen if they fail to take care of themselves. Explain the possible outcomes of negligence; they will find the solutions on their own.

If it sounds like you are giving unsolicited advice, switch to the storytelling technique. Narrate your past experiences when you should have prioritized healthcare and ended up with more problems than before. In fact, you should avoid giving unsolicited advice in all aspects of their life.

They have become mature enough to select their career path on their own. It may differ from their childhood dreams but don't keep reminding them about the change. Don't add to their confusion. Help them navigate their career challenges if they ask for it. If not, simply show your support; that is all they need to accomplish their goals.

The same goes for deciding on their romantic partner. You may have an idealized version of their spouse, but the decision is theirs to make. It shouldn't matter if they choose someone from a different religion, country, race, or sex. It should not be your concern even if they choose multiple partners or stay with one person their whole life. If you wish to be privy to their romantic lives, you need to show your support of their choice.

Failures form a part of this cycle, too. If your adult children don't want you to interfere when they are going through a breakup, a divorce, an unexpected pregnancy, a professional or academic setback, or any kind of failure, let them be, but at the same time, also let them know you are there for them. Show your support, let them realize you understand what they are going through, but don't criticize their actions. Keep checking in with them occasionally, and seek professional help if the need arises.

Finally, celebrating traditional activities is an effective way to strengthen healthy relationships with your adult children. Encourage the whole family to join in planning family traditions. Let them share their ideas and preferences and incorporate their input into the tradition-making process.

Adapt traditions to their changing circumstances. Accommodate their schedules, preferences, and life stages. For instance, organize adult-specific games like Secret Santa instead of perpetuating the pretense that Santa Claus gave them gifts during Christmas. Flexibility ensures that traditions remain relevant and inclusive for everyone involved. Alternatively, you may also create new traditions together.

Consistency is key to the success of family traditions. Make an effort to enjoy traditions regularly, whether weekly, monthly, or annually. If distance separates you from your adult children, leverage technology to stay connected and participate in traditions together.

Encourage active participation from all family members in traditions, not just your adult children. Give everyone a part to play in planning and execution, and create opportunities for meaningful and joyful engagement to foster a sense of belonging in the traditions.

During your gatherings, reflect on shared memories and experiences associated with family traditions. Reminisce about past traditions, share stories, and create opportunities for nostalgia to strengthen familial bonds and create a sense of continuity across generations. At the same time, recognize that family dynamics and traditions may evolve, and be open to embracing change when necessary.

The ultimate goal of parenting is to raise independent, responsible adults. When your children grow up, your parenting role does not end. It evolves. If you embrace this change, you can maintain and even deepen a loving relationship with your young adult children.

Key Takeaways

- Accept the changing dynamic as an essential and natural part of your child's growth.
- Foster open communication without imposing opinions.
- Be supportive but respect their autonomy—offer advice when asked.
- Set boundaries—respect privacy but provide unconditional love and support.
- Let them know you are always there for them

Trust them—trust in their ability to make sound decisions and believe that they are capable of coping with challenges thrown at them.

REFERENCES

Agnihotri, A. (2022, August 22). Ways to improve your teen's mental wellness. Hindustan Times. https://www.hindustantimes.com/lifestyle/health/ways-to-improve-your-teen-s-mental-wellness-101661152399209.html

Bernstein, Jeffrey. "3 Reasons Why Adult Children May Treat Their Parents like Dirt | Psychology Today United Kingdom." Www.psychologytoday.com, 6 Mar. 2023, www.psychologytoday.com/gb/blog/liking-the-child-you-love/202303/3-reasons-your-adult-child-treats-you-like-dirt. Accessed 4 Mar. 2024.

Borresen, K. (2023, October 4). Want A Better Relationship With Your Adult Children? Do These 6 Things. HuffPost. https://www.huffpost.com/entry/better-relationship-adult-children-parent_l_651c3cdfe4b0b443172fd98e

Budgeting for Teens: Teaching Teens to Save. (n.d.). RegionsBank. https://www.regions.com/insights/personal/personal-finances/budgeting-and-saving/teaching-teens-how-to-save-money

Burns, Dr. Jim. "What to Do When Your Adult Child Is Messing Up." Parent Cue, 1 June 2020, theparentcue.org/what-to-do-when-your-adult-child-is-messing-up/. Accessed 4 Mar. 2024.

Champion. (2022, June 15). Why Teens Need Self Care. Champion Your Parenting. https://www.championyourparenting.com/why-teens-need-self-care/

Chen, X. (2021). The Impact of Child-Parent Relationship on Young Adults' Career Choice Terms of Use. https://dash.harvard.edu/bitstream/handle/1/37370040/ThesisFinal_Chen

Cherry, Kendra. "How to Improve Your Communication in Relationships." Verywell Mind, 23 Feb. 2022, www.verywellmind.com/communication-in-relationships-why-it-matters-and-how-to-improve-5218269.

ChristineXP, & ChristineXP. (2024, January 25). 10 Things Every Teen Should Know About Dealing with a Mental Health Issue. Discovery Mood & Anxiety Program. https://discoverymood.com/blog/10-tips-teen-dealing-with-a-mental-health/

Crossfield, Alisa. "Why Your Teen Feels like All You Do Is Criticize Them and How to Fix It." Parentingteensandtweens.com, 6 June 2023, parentingteensandtweens.com/why-your-teen-feels-like-all-you-do-is-criticize-them-and-how-to-fix-it/. Accessed 6 Mar. 2024.

D'Amico, P. (2019, October 31). What Common Challenges Are Young Adults Facing Today? Paradigm Treatment. https://paradigmtreatment.com/challenges-young-adults-facing-today/

Davenport, C. R., & Psy, D. (2022, May 6). How to handle conflict with your adult children. Davenportpsychology.com; Davenport Psychology. https://davenportpsychology.com/2022/05/06/how-to-handle-conflict-with-your-adult-children

Donnan. (2021, August 3). How To Support Your Teen or Young Adult Job Seeker. Donnan Coaching Serv. https://www.donnancoachingservices.com/post/how-to-support-your-teen-or-young-adult-jobseeker

8 tips for teaching teens how to save money | MoneySense. (2023, December 21). MoneySense. https://natwest.mymoneysense.com/parents/articles/8-tips-for-teaching-teens-how-to-save-money/

Eketone, Sheridan. "Raising Great Adults: Why Teens Need Autonomy." Parenting Place, parentingplace.nz/resources/raising-great-adults-why-teens-need-autonomy. Accessed 6 Mar. 2024.

Extra Mile. (2019, November 4). Adult children. Thehartford.com. https://extramile.thehartford.com/family/parenting/parenting-adult-children/

Fitness and Your 13- to 18-Year-Old (for Parents). (n.d.). Nemours KidsHealth. https://kidshealth.org/en/parents/fitness-13-18.html

Gelke, Cynthia. "Being a Parent to a Young Adult | Sutter Health." Www.sutterhealth.org, July 2019, www.sutterhealth.org/health/young-adults/relationships-social-skills/parenting-a-young-adult.

Gregory, Lauren. "Autonomy in Child Development." Mybrightwheel.com, 7 Apr. 2023, mybrightwheel.com/blog/autonomy-child-development.

Han, Christina S, et al. "Parental Autonomy Support in the Context of Parent–Child Negotiation for Children's Independent Mobility: "I Always Feel Safer with My Parents" to "Boom! Bust down Those Walls!"" The Journal of Early Adolescence, vol. 42, no. 6, 6 Jan. 2022, pp. 737–764, https://doi.org/10.1177/02724316211064513.

Investing basics for teens. (2023, May 11). https://www.fidelity.com/learning-center/personal-finance/teach-teens-investing

Isaac, V. (2014, March 13). How to help your child navigate a route to career success. The Guardian. https://www.theguardian.com/careers/how-help-child-navigate-career-paths

Jain, T., & Joshi, P. (2021). The Stage of Young Adulthood: Challenges and Issues in Career Choices. The Stage of Young Adulthood: Challenges and Issues in Career Choices, 9(2). https://doi.org/10.25215/0902.201

Jones, D. (2024, February 18). How to Help Your Teen Explore Possible Careers: 15 Steps.

Joyner, L. (2023, August 20). 5 Ways to Help Your Young Adult Children Make Smarter Choices: Guidance for Parenting the Transitioning Generation. Hustle Mama Magazine. https://hustlemamamagazine.com/5-ways-to-help-your-young-adult-children-make-smarter-choices-guidance-for-parenting-the-transitioning-generation/

Kessler, Owen. "26 Examples of Healthy Boundaries in a Relationship." Marriage Advice - Expert Marriage Tips & Advice, 28 Nov. 2023, www.marriage.com/advice/marriage-fitness/examples-of-healthy-boundaries-in-relationship/. Accessed 2 Mar. 2024.

Lcsw, A. M. (2020, March 6). Steps to Good Decision Making Skills for Teens. Verywell Family. https://www.verywellfamily.com/steps-to-good-decision-making-skills-for-teens-2609104

Martins, Julia. "How to Give and Take Constructive Criticism • Asana." Asana, 18 July 2022, asana.com/resources/constructive-criticism.

McClure, R. (2005, September 29). How to create quality time with your family. Verywell Family. https://www.verywellfamily.com/finding-quality-family-time-616982

McDermott, Nicole. "How to Communicate in a Relationship, according to Experts." Forbes Health, 25 Aug. 2022, www.forbes.com/health/wellness/how-to-communicate-in-a-relationship/.

Medvec, S. (2015, January 29). Fixing a broken relationship with your adult child. The Summit Counseling Center. https://summitcounseling.org/fixing-a-broken-relationship-with-your-adult-child/

millennialmarketingag. (2023, June 9). Teaching Teenagers About Taxes: A Helpful Guide for Parents. JRJ Income Tax Service. https://jrjtax.com/2023/06/teaching-teenagers-about-taxes-a-helpful-guide-for-parents/

Miranda. (2020, February 19). 12 Smart Ways to Help Your Teenager Choose a Career Path. The Reluctant Cowgirl. https://thereluctantcowgirl.com/help-teenager-choose-a-career-path/

Paris, W. B. D. (2022, September 19). Debt 101: A Guide for Parents and Teenagers | Mydoh. Mydoh. https://www.mydoh.ca/learn/money-101/debt/debt-101-a-guide-for-parents-and-teenagers/

Pattemore, Chantelle. "10 Ways to Build and Preserve Better Boundaries." Psych Central, 3 June 2021, psychcentral.com/lib/10-way-to-build-and-preserve-better-boundaries.

Rd, T. L. (2020, May 4). How to Talk to Teens About Healthy Eating - The Whole U. The Whole U. https://thewholeu.uw.edu/2020/03/25/how-to-talk-about-healthy-eating-with-teens/

Resolving conflict with your adult child. (n.d.). Org.au. Retrieved March 8, 2024, from https://www.raq.org.au/blog/resolving-conflict-your-adult-child

Ritter, S. (2019, June 17). How To Help Your Teenager Deal With Setbacks In Life» Daily Mom. Daily Mom. https://dailymom.com/nurture/setbacks-in-life-parenting-teens/

Robinson, R. (2023, August 8). Family estrangement: 6 ways to reconcile with adult children. Focus on the Family. https://www.focusonthefamily.com/parenting/family-estrangement-6-ways-to-reconcile-with-adult-children/

Russell, Dr Lucy. "Helping Your Child Cope with Setbacks." They Are the Future, 14 June 2023, www.theyarethefuture.co.uk/helping-child-cope-setbacks/.

Ryan, Emily. "Mentoring Means Sharing Experience rather than Giving Advice." Mentorloop Mentoring Software, 30 Jan. 2023, mentorloop.com/blog/share-experience/#:~:text=The%20Difference%20Between%20Giving%20Advice%20and%20Sharing%20Experiences. Accessed 6 Mar. 2024.

Stoltzfus, Dr Jack. "Parents - Learn to Listen More Effectively to Your Young Adult." Parents Letting Go - Dr. Jack Stoltzfus, 19 Feb. 2021, parentslettinggo.com/parents-learn-to-listen-more-effectively-to-your-young-adult/. Accessed 6 Mar. 2024.

Stoltzfus, Dr Jack. "Parents of Young Adults: Why We Suffer." Parents Letting Go - Dr. Jack Stoltzfus, 20 June 2022, parentslettinggo.com/parents-of-young-adults-why-we-suffer/. Accessed 2 Mar. 2024.

Suni, E., & Suni, E. (2023, October 4). Teens and Sleep. Sleep Foundation. https://www.sleepfoundation.org/teens-and-sleep

10 Ways to Manage Everyday Stress (for Teens). (n.d.). Nemours KidsHealth. https://kidshealth.org/en/teens/stress-tips.html

The Foundations Team. (2021, February 16). Trusting your Young Adult to Make and Learn from Mistakes. Foundations Asheville. https://foundationsasheville.com/blog/trusting-your-young-adult-to-make-and-learn-from-mistakes/

thetherapistparent. "Helping Children Grow through Set Backs." The Therapist Parent, 5 Apr. 2022, www.thetherapistparent.com/post/helping-children-grow-through-set-backs. Accessed 4 Mar. 2024.

Thomas, Patricia A, et al. "Family Relationships and Well-Being." Innovation in Aging, vol. 1, no. 3, 11 Nov. 2017, pp. 1–11, www.ncbi.nlm.nih.gov/pmc/articles/PMC5954612/, https://doi.org/10.1093/geroni/igx025.

Thomson, E. (2023, September 12). How to Communicate Better with Your Young Adult. PrairieCare. https://prairie-care.com/resources/type/blog/how-to-communicate-better-with-your-young-adult/

Try this to manage conflicts with your adult child. (n.d.). Psychology Today. Retrieved March 8, 2024, from https://www.psychologytoday.com/intl/blog/liking-the-child-you-love/202207/try-manage-conflicts-your-adult-child

Tumuramye, D. (2022, August 31). How to prioritize time with your family. The Observer - Uganda. https://observer.ug/viewpoint/74961-how-to-prioritize-time-with-your-family

Turner, B. (2011, May 4). 5 ways to stay in touch with your grown children. HowStuffWorks. https://lifestyle.howstuffworks.com/family/parenting/parenting-tips/5-ways-to-stay-in-touch-with-grown-children.htm

Waters, Shonna. "Healthy Boundaries in Relationships: A Guide for Building and Keeping." Www.betterup.com, 13 Apr. 2022, www.betterup.com/blog/healthy-boundaries-in-relationships.

White, J., & Weeden, L. (2004, January 1). Help Your Teen Deal With Setbacks. Focus on the Family. https://www.focusonthefamily.com/parenting/help-your-teen-deal-with-setbacks/

Wonders, Lynn. "Parenting Young Adult Children." Wonders Counseling Services, LLC, 13 Sept. 2015, wonderscounseling.com/when-your-children-become-young-adults/. Accessed 2 Mar. 2024.

"Active Listening | Communicating | Essentials | Parenting Information | CDC." Www.cdc.gov, 23 Jan. 2023, www.cdc.gov/parents/essentials/toddlersandpreschoolers/communication/activelistening.html#:~:text=Active%20listening%20is%20a%20good.

"Why Active Listening Is Important in Parent-Child Relationships." Www.familycentre.org, 1 Mar. 2022, www.familycentre.org/news/post/why-active-listening-is-important-in-parent-child-relationships.

Printed in Dunstable, United Kingdom